Robert Cochrane

Lives and discoveries of famous travellers

Robert Cochrane

Lives and discoveries of famous travellers

ISBN/EAN: 9783337206017

Printed in Europe, USA, Canada, Australia, Japan

Cover: Foto ©Andreas Hilbeck / pixelio.de

More available books at **www.hansebooks.com**

LIVES AND DISCOVERIES

OF

FAMOUS TRAVELLERS.

Compiled by the Editor of

'THE ENGLISH CIRCUMNAVIGATORS,' 'THE ENGLISH EXPLORERS,' 'THE TREASURY
OF MODERN BIOGRAPHY,' ETC.

DAVID LIVINGSTONE, LL.D., D.C.L.
SIR SAMUEL WHITE BAKER.
HENRY M. STANLEY.
MAJOR SERPA PINTO.

FIFTH THOUSAND.

NEW YORK:
R. WORTHINGTON,
770 BROADWAY.
1883.

PREFATORY NOTE.

THE following accounts of the Lives and Discoveries of several distinguished modern Travellers form another volume in the list of popular works, issued by the Publishers with the view of meeting the steadily increasing demand for reading of a wholesome and instructive character. The details in each case, for each narrative, have been drawn directly from the original sources of information,—Dr. Livingstone's *Missionary Travels;* Sir Samuel Baker's *Albert Nyanza* and *Ismailia;* Mr. H. M. Stanley's *Across the Dark Continent;* and for Major Pinto's travels, the letter submitted to Lord Northbrook, President of the Royal Geographical Society.

CONTENTS.

LIVES AND DISCOVERIES OF
FAMOUS TRAVELLERS.

DAVID LIVINGSTONE, LL.D., D.C.L.

THE facts in the early life of Livingstone, though familiar enough, have an undying interest to the student of biography. In a character which embraced so many simple, sincere, and earnest elements, there is a danger of overlooking his simple, manly greatness. His great-grandfather fell at the battle of Culloden; his grandfather was a small farmer in Ulva, where Neil Livingstone, his father, was born, and his youth was nurtured amongst the traditionary legends of a past age. David Livingstone was born at Blantyre, near Glasgow, in 1813.

Livingstone relates that his grandfather could give particulars of the lives of his ancestors for six generations. One of these traditions told of a hardy islander, who, on his death-bed, called his children round him, and said, 'Now, in my lifetime, I have searched most carefully through all the traditions I could find of our family, and I never could discover that there was a dishonest man among our forefathers. If, therefore, any of you, or any of your children, should take to dishonest ways, it will not be because it runs in our blood; it does not belong to you. I leave this precept with you, " Be honest!"' Like many of the Highlanders, his ancestors were Roman Catholics; but he says 'they were made Protestants by the laird coming round with a man having a yellow staff, which would seem to have attracted more attention than his teaching, for the new religion went long afterwards, perhaps it does so still, by the name of "the religion of the yellow stick."'

The island of Ulva yielding insufficient support for a numerous family, his grandfather had removed to Blantyre Works, situated on the Clyde, near Glasgow. His sons were received as clerks in the factory there. His uncles entered the army or navy, but his father remained at home, carrying on the business of a small tea-dealer, but was, as his son remarks, too conscientious to become rich. They were members of the Church of Scotland, a religious establishment which he speaks of as having been an incalculable blessing to the country. During the last twenty years of his life, however, he went to an Independent church in Hamilton, where he held the office of deacon. Livingstone revered his father's memory, and spoke of him as presenting to his family a continuously consistent, pious example. His mother he remembered as an anxious housewife, striving to make both ends meet.

David Livingstone, at the age of ten, was sent to the factory as a 'piecer,' to help the household income. Part of his first week's wages he expended in buying Ruddiman's *Rudiments of Latin.* The study of Latin he vigorously pursued at an evening school, which met between the hours

of eight and ten at night. Not unfrequently he would continue his studies till twelve o'clock, although he had to be
at the factory by six o'clock in the morning till eight in the
evening, with intervals for breakfast and dinner. He said,
in writing his *Missionary Travels*, that he knew *Virgil* and
Horace better in these early days than he did at that time.
In addition he read everything he could lay his hands on,
except novels. Works of travel, or books relating to scientific
research, were his favourites; and with his limited leisure
he managed to make himself acquainted with the scenery,
botany, and geology of his native district. He had a habit
of fixing upon the spinning-jenny the book he was reading,
so that his eye could catch the sentence as he passed on
his work. His father, with a narrowness of mind character-
istic of many good men in his position, would have preferred
that he should have been poring over such works as the
Cloud of Witnesses, or Boston's *Fourfold State*, to reading
such miscellaneous literature. In the fresh glow of Christian
ardour, Livingstone determined upon becoming a medical
missionary to China, and began to turn his mind towards
preparation for the mission field.

Livingstone was promoted to the more laborious toil of
a cotton spinner while in his nineteenth year, and he was
thus enabled to support himself while attending the medical,
Greek, and Divinity classes in Glasgow. ' I never,' he wrote,
' received a farthing of aid from any one, and should have
accomplished my project of going to China as a medical
missionary in the course of time by my own efforts, had
not some friends advised my joining the London Missionary
Society, on account of its perfectly unsectarian character.
It sends neither Episcopacy, nor Presbyterianism, nor Inde-

pendency, but the Gospel of Christ to the heathen.   This exactly agreed with my ideas of what a missionary society ought to do; but it was not without a pang that I offered myself, for it was not quite agreeable to one accustomed to work his own way to become, in a measure, dependent on others.   And I would not have been much put about though my offer had been rejected.'   When properly qualified to carry out his original plan, the opium war was raging in China, so he found it inexpedient to go there.   Turning his thoughts to Africa, where Moffat was labouring, he went through a more extended theological course in England than he had previously done in Glasgow.   In 1840, after a preliminary examination, he was ordained as a medical missionary by the London Missionary Society.   He sailed for the Cape, after a brief stay at which he landed at Port Natal, and soon made personal acquaintance at Kuruman with the Rev. Robert Moffat, whose daughter he afterwards married.

After remaining at Kuruman and the neighbourhood for a few months, Livingstone took up his quarters in the Backwain country at Lepelóle; and cutting himself off from all inter-course with Europeans for six months, devoted himself to acquiring an insight into the habits, ways of thinking, laws, and language of the Bechuanas, and in laying the foundations of a settlement by making a canal for irrigation purposes from a river near by.   He visited the Bakaa, Bamangwato, and the Makalaka, living between 22° and 23° south latitude. Obliged to leave the country of the Backwains, he settled in the valley of Mabotsa, the home of the Makatla branch of the Bechuana tribe.   The place was infested with lions, which would attack the herds sometimes in broad daylight.

It was in this neighbourhood that Livingstone had the memorable encounter with the lion, when the bone of his left arm was crushed into splinters. After labouring earnestly for some time among the Makatla, he visited Cape Town in 1844, and during his visit was married to Moffat's eldest daughter. In 1845 they set up house at Skokuane, then the headquarters of the Backwain chief Sechele, who, although a rain-maker, helped forward the work of the noble-hearted missionary, and even proposed to convert his people in a body through the agency of whips made of rhinoceros hide. The description which Livingstone gave of the belief of the white man, and of 'the great white throne, and Him who shall sit on it,' caused this chief to exclaim, 'You startle me. These words make all my bones to shake. I have no more strength in me. But my forefathers were living at the same time as yours were, and how is it they did not send them word about these terrible things sooner? They all passed into darkness without knowing whither they were going.' His early efforts among the Backwains were greatly retarded by a drought, which lasted three years, and which was partly attributed to Livingstone's influence over Sechele, their rain-maker and chief.

The exertions of those explorers who preceded David Livingstone, however useful, were mostly limited to the Kaffir regions; and it was not till the time of Livingstone that any attempt was made to pass what is called the desert of Kalahari, comprehending the space from the Orange river, in south latitude 29°, to Lake Ngami in the north, and from about 24° east longitude to near the west coast. Dr. Livingstone formed the resolution to pass this desert; and from 1849 he was engaged in carrying that resolution into effect.

The region of the desert is occupied by the Bakalahari and the Bushmen, who prey upon the game, chiefly antelopes, which require only a scanty supply of water, and feed upon the grass and numerous tuberous plants. The start was made in June, and the party proceeded without interruption. They came on the second day to Serotli, where the country is flat, and composed of white sand. After passing the salt-pan district of Ncho-kotsa, where the play of the mirage on the salt incrustations deceived them into the belief that the reservoirs were lakes, they came to the river Zouga, running to the north-east, and described by the people as coming out of the Lake Ngami. The people of this district possess a language which shows that they are connected by lineage with the north. On ascending the river, described as beauti-fully wooded, they found a large stream flowing into it called the Tamunak'le. The information received that this stream came from a country of rivers, first suggested to Dr. Living-stone that there might be a highway capable of being traversed by boats to an unexplored region; and when the party came to the lake, this idea became so predominant that it seemed to diminish the value of the actual discovery. The lake, supposed to be about seventy miles in circumference, is shallow, and never can be of much commercial importance. Dr. Livingstone returned to Kolobeng. His next purpose was to go up the Tamunak'le and visit Sebituane, the chief of the Makololo, who live in the swamps between the Chobe and the Zambesi. In June 1851 he saw, in the centre of the continent, the Zambesi itself, which was not previously known to exist there at all; and having come to a resolution to ascend it from Sesheke, he subsequently made the necessary preparations. He collected canoes to the number of thirty-three, with about 160 men. They went rapidly along, admiring the beauty of the banks, a mile asunder, and the many islands finely wooded. The occurrence of cataracts forced them at times to carry their canoes; but they soon made their way to the Barotse valley, a hundred miles in length, and bearing a resemblance to that of the Nile, with its capital, Naliele, erected on an eminence. Up to Libonta the river presents the appearance of low banks without trees; but twenty miles beyond that the forest comes down to the water's edge, and along with it the plague of Africa—the tsetse, a fly whose bite is fatal to domestic oxen, and to no other animals. Having at length arrived at Ma-Sekelutu, the chief who accompanied the expedition resolved to return, and the party accordingly made again for Sesheke. The Doctor having failed to discover a healthy place for a settlement, now determined on endeavouring to open a path to the west coast. This he put into execution by what may be called his third journey. In this he reached the junction of the Loeti and the Zambesi, and having returned to Linyanti, he started for the west coast. Reaching the confluence of the Leeba with the Zambesi, he crossed the Quango, and arrived at Loanda. On his return to Linyanti, once more he visited the falls called Victoria, arrived at the Tete, and finally at Quilimane, on the east coast.

Dr. Livingstone had thus laid open a wide zone, comprehending the country of rivers; but as the Zambesi was fed by large streams from the north, it was necessary that these should be explored. One of these, the Shiré, he ascended by means of a small steamer in 1859. He found it a stream with a breadth of 160 yards, and a depth of ten or twelve feet. By this means he was led to the Shirwah, a lake two

hundred miles long and fifty broad, with an elevation above
the sea-level of 1800 feet, and, like the Tanganyika, surrounded by verdant mountains, whereof one, Mount Zumba,
is 7000 feet high.   In the vicinity of this the members of the
mission were located.   Fish, leeches, alligators, and sea-cows
abound in the lake, the water of which is brackish.

In August 1861 Dr. Livingstone and his party proceeded
to explore another lake called Nyassa, by ascending farther
the Shiré, and passing through a valley with many villages
and plantations.   Coming to a series of rapids called Murchison Cataracts, they were obliged to carry a four-oared boat
for a period of three weeks to get again to the navigable part
of the river.   These cataracts extend over thirty-five miles of
latitude, with a total fall, from the first to the last, of 1200
feet.   These obstacles having been surmounted, the travellers
again launched their boat in the upper parts of the Shiré, and
soon thereafter they found themselves floating on the Nyassa
Lake, or, as it is sometimes called, the Star Lake, the western
shores of which they explored for two hundred miles, partly
by the banks on foot, and partly by the boat.

This lake they found to be exposed to frequent storms, so
violent that the party could not venture far from the shore ;
yet they got some rough measurements by triangulation at
those places where the opposite bank could be seen.   The lake
is represented as having something of the boot shape of Italy,
being narrowest at the ankle, where it is 20 miles across ;
its average breadth is 38 miles, and its length 350 miles.   It
is estimated as lying 1500 feet above the sea-level, and being
about 350 miles from the coast of Mozambique.   The party
could learn nothing as to its northern extremity, but it was supposed to extend beyond the parallel of the tenth degree south,

its southern extremity being in the fourteenth degree. It is surrounded by low marshy plains, frequented by water-fowl, and forming a haunt for the elephant and other wild beasts. Beyond, at a distance of eight miles, were seen ranges of granite hills covered with wood. The party estimated the depth of the lake by the colour of the water; near the shore it is bright green, and towards the centre a deep blue, like the colour of the sea. Within a mile of the shore a sounding line of 200 fathoms failed to reach the bottom. The temperature of the water was 72° Fahrenheit, and the fish were plentiful. It was further observed that the lake is fed by many streams, no fewer than twelve having been crossed by the party as they proceeded on the west side; and the consequence is that during the rainy season the waters rise sometimes to the extent of three feet.

The natives inhabiting the country to the south of the lake are of one tribe and one language, rearing their villages so close together that they form a continuous line. They are of a superior class of negroes, good cultivators of the soil, and hardy fishermen. Like most of the people in the countries traversed by the party, those in this region were civil to the strangers, and exacted no tribute. The slave trade, which seems to embrace all regions occupied by the negro, was found here to be carried on with activity, there being even a boat called a *dhow* ready for carrying the victims from one side to the other.

Thus was another of the African problems solved; for although Portuguese travellers had mentioned that there was a lake in this quarter, and even given it a name, Maravi, according to which it figures in some old maps, yet the accounts were so vague and valueless that the lake did not appear in the more modern maps. Other problems remained, such as the origin of the Rovuma river, which fell into the Indian Ocean about the tenth degree of southern latitude. At this time Dr. Livingstone and a party went up it thirty miles, but the waters began to fall so rapidly that they were obliged to return.

In the Nyassa district traces of the odious slave trade were everywhere met with in the shape of ruined villages, broken utensils, and human skeletons. The extent of the slave trade in this district was borne out by the fact that 19,000 slaves passed through the custom-house of the island of Zanzibar at that time.

On the 27th April 1862, Mrs. Livingstone died from the effects of climate at Shupanga, on the Zambesi, where she was buried. The Rev. James Stewart of the Free Church of Scotland read the service over the grave. Livingstone now employed himself in exploring the Rovuma, which he found to have two feeders—one from the south-west, rising in the mountains of Nyassa, the other from the west-north-west. He next continued his researches on the Zambesi and Shiré. In January 1863, the *Pioneer* steamed up the Shiré with the *Lady Nyassa* in tow. Traces of the dreadful results of a slave raid were everywhere visible. The miserable inhabitants who had been spared were in a state of semi-starvation. Dead bodies were frequently met in the huts 'with the poor rags round the loins, the skull fallen off the pillow; the little skeleton of the child, that had perished first, rolled up in a mat between two large skeletons.' Mr. Thornton, geologist of the expedition, died here, after assisting Baron Vanderdecken in a survey of the Kilimanjaro Mountains; the height of the highest member of the range has since been proved to be

18,700 feet, and the height of a companion peak, only by a little overtopping the line of perpetual snow, to be 2500 feet lower.

While engaged in making a road through the forest to connect the lower Shiré with the upper, the Rev. Charles Livingstone and Dr. John Kirk, after having been repeatedly seized with fever and dysentery, were obliged to part from Livingstone on the 19th of May 1863, and return home. Only two months later he received a despatch from Lord John Russell, Minister for Foreign Affairs, withdrawing the expedition. In accordance with these instructions, he proceeded to the mouth of the Zambesi and to Zanzibar, and navigating the vessel himself, sailed for Bombay, a distance of over 2500 miles. He then disposed of his vessel, the *Lady Nyassa,* for £2000. Unfortunately, soon after this money was committed to the hands of a Bombay banker, he became bankrupt, and the whole sum was lost. On his return to England in 1864, Livingstone would have retired from active service. Sir Roderick Murchison had asked him to name a leader for a new expedition to explore the watershed between Nyassa and Tanganyika. The eminent traveller who had been asked refused, and Sir Roderick appealed to Livingstone, and overruled any objections he had to make.

On the 14th August 1865, with recruited health, and after having superintended the publication of his explorations on the Zambesi, the Shiré, the Rovuma, and Lake Nyassa, he began to make preparations for a new expedition. Sir Roderick Murchison, president of the Geographical Society, requested him this time to undertake the exploration of the intermediate country lying between Northern Nyassa and Tanganyika. Earl Russell renewed Livingstone's appointment as H.M. Consul to the tribes in the interior. Mr. James

Young of Kelly, one of his oldest friends, subscribed £1000 to further this expedition, and £500 was given by the Government, and another £500 by the Royal Geographical Society for a like purpose.

He set out from England on the 14th August 1865, accompanied by his daughter Agnes as far as Paris, thence proceeding alone direct to Bombay. The Government of that Presidency assisted him with a supply of arms and other necessaries for the expedition. He also secured the services of Chuma, Wakatani, Edward Gardner, Simon Price, and other Zambesi liberated slaves who were being educated in a Nassick school there. Having supplied the other necessary requirements for his explorations, he sailed from Bombay to Zanzibar. At Zanzibar the British Consul, Dr. G. E. Seward, did all in his power to further the expedition.

On the 19th March 1866, he sailed from Zanzibar for Mikindany Bay, a deep indentation in the East African coast, about twenty miles north of the river Rovuma, and about five degrees of latitude south of the island of Zanzibar. His expedition consisted of Dr. Livingstone himself, ten natives of Johanna, engaged by Mr. Sunley the English Consul, thirteen natives of the Zambesi, and thirteen Sepoys of the Bombay Marine—altogether thirty-seven souls. The only European of the party was Dr. Livingstone. The animals taken with him were six camels, four buffaloes, four asses, and two mules, with which he had resolved he should experiment as to their adaptability for African travelling.

Livingstone and his party started for the interior in a southwesterly direction, with the intention of crossing the Rovuma to reach the north end of Lake Nyassa. A few letters reached the coast for friends at home, informing them how he was succeeding in his journey. Then there came a long pause, to be broken, however, in December 1866, by the sad intelligence of his murder by a predatory band of the Mazitu.

'After some deliberation,' says a leading journalist, 'Sir Roderick Murchison and the Geographical Society entreated the Government to equip a boat expedition to proceed to Lake Nyassa, to discover the truth of the report, as there were a great many influential people in England who, like Sir Roderick, doubted, for several reasons, the veracity of Musa.

'This boat expedition was entrusted to Mr. E. D. Young, a warrant-officer of the Royal Navy, and Lieutenant Faulkner of the 17th Lancers, and departed from England on the 11th June for the Zambesi. Arriving at that river, a portable steel boat, built in sections, was put together, and the first search expedition after Livingstone started for the Shiré.

'At Chibisa's, below the Murchison Cataracts of the Shiré, the steel boat was disconnected, thence carried overland a distance of forty miles, then launched on the quiet waters of the upper Shiré, up which the party sailed for the Nyassa Lake. Mr. Young proved conclusively that, though no member of the expedition saw the traveller, Dr. Livingstone was not murdered anywhere near the locality mentioned by Musa. The natives round about solemnly averred that he had gone to the west in good condition and health. At Marenga the people said that the Johanna men had returned to their village but two days after they had departed from the lake in company with the Doctor, and that, when they were asked why they had returned, they replied that they had simply agreed to take him so far, and therefore were at liberty to return. This was at least confirmatory evidence

that the Johanna men had lied; that they had only concocted
their tragic tale after their departure from Nyassa in order
to obtain their pay from the Consul.

'In 1868, however, letters came from Livingstone himself,
dated at Bemba, February 1867, wherein he explained that
he had been unable to send despatches before, owing to the
absence of caravans in the new lands he had traversed.'

On the 18th of July 1868, Livingstone had seen, for the
first time, the shores of Lake Bemba, or Bangweolo, which
had never before been visited by a European. The country
around the lake was all flat, and very much denuded of trees,
except the motsikiri, or mosikisi, which has fine, dark, dense
foliage, and is spared for its shade and the fatty oil yielded
by its seeds. The bottom of the lake consisted of fine white
sand, and a broad belt of strong rushes, about a hundred
yards wide, shows shallow water. The innumerable springs
in the neighbourhood of this lake Dr. Livingstone looked
upon as the primary or ultimate sources of the Zambesi,
Congo, and Nile. In his supposition regarding the latter he
was, however, mistaken.

In October of the same year, Livingstone had made his
way to Kalongosi. At Kabwabwata, some of his old servants
who had previously deserted returned to him. An outbreak
of war among the native tribes detained him here for some
time. He was now endeavouring to reach Ujiji. Early in
1869, a dangerous illness left evils behind it from which he
never fully recovered. In January he had to be carried.
On 14th February he again reached Tanganyika. The cough
and chest pain from which he was suffering now diminished,
although he was greatly emaciated. On the 17th November
he reached the Luamo river (200 yards wide). In January

1870, Livingstone again suffered from sickness and choleraic symptoms. In July he was terribly troubled by irritable eating ulcers, which had again fastened on his feet.

While at Nyangwe, Manyuema, Mr. Stanley said he found, on diligent inquiries, that 'Livingstone's residence, his travels hither and thither, and his journeys from and to Ujiji, must have embraced a period of three years or thereabouts. The distance from Ujiji to Nyangwe is about 350 English miles, which we performed in forty days, inclusive of halts. I find he was laid up a very long time with a most painful disease of the feet at Kabambarre. From native accounts he seems to have been there from six to twelve months. The traveller "Daoud," or David, is a well-remembered figure in this region between Nyangwe and the Tanganyika. He has made an impression on the people which will not be forgotten for a generation at least. "Did you know him?" old Mwana Ngoi of the Luama asked of me eagerly. Upon receiving an affirmative, he said to his sons and brothers, "Do you hear what he says? He knew the good white man. Ah! we shall hear all about him." Then, turning to me, he asked me, "Was he not a very good man?" to which I replied, "Yes, my friend; he was good: far better than any man, white or Arab, you will ever see again." "Ah! yes; you speak true. He has saved me from being robbed many a time by the Arabs, and he was so gentle and patient, and told us such pleasant stories of the wonderful land of the white people. Hm', the aged white, was a good man indeed!" Had old Mwana Ngoi been able to speak as an educated person, I should no doubt have had something like a narrative of David Livingstone's virtues from him; whereas, not being educated, much of what he said was broken by frequent *hm's* and shakings of his head, as though the traveller's good qualities were beyond description or enumeration. He wisely left the rest to my imagination, and so I leave them to you. But what has struck me, while tracing Livingstone to his utmost reach — this Arab depot of Nyangwe—revived all my grief and pity for him, greater, indeed, than even his own relation of sorrowful and heavy things, is that he does not seem to have been aware that he was sacrificing himself unnecessarily, nor submit to be warned of the havoc of age, and of the little power left him. With the weight of many years pressing on him, the shortest march wearying him, compelling him to halt many days to recover his strength, a serious attack of illness frequently prostrating him, with neither men nor means to obtain proper escort and enable him to make practical progress, Livingstone was at last like a blind and infirm man, aimlessly moving about. From my conscience—with not a whit of my admiration and love for him lessened in the smallest degree, but rather increased by what I have heard from Arabs and natives —I must say I think his very hardest taskmaster was himself.'

The natives of Bambarré and Manyuema he found to be very superstitious. On the 18th August he made the following notes in his journal at Bambarré :—

'I learn from Josut and Moenepembé, who have been to Katanga and beyond, that there is a lake N.N.W. of the copper mines, and twelve days distant. It is called Chibungo, and is said to be large. Seven days west of Katanga flows another Lualaba, the dividing line between Rua and Lunda or Londa. It is very large, and, as the Lufira flows into Chibungo, it is probable that the Lualaba West and Lufira form the lake. Lualaba West and Lufira rise by fountains south of Katanga, three or four days off. Luambai and Lunga fountains are only about ten miles distant from Lualaba West and Dufira fountains: a mound rises between them, the most remarkable in Africa. Were this spot in Armenia, it would serve exactly the description of the garden of Eden in Genesis, with its four rivers—the Gihon, Pison, Hiddekel, and Euphrates. As it is, it possibly gave occasion to the story told to Herodotus by the secretary of Minerva in the city of Saïs, about two hills with conical tops, Crophi and Mophi. "Midway between them," said he, "are the fountains of the Nile, fountains which it is impossible to fathom; half the water runs northward into Egypt, half to the south towards Ethiopia."

'Four fountains rising so near to each other would readily be supposed to have one source, and half the water flowing into the Nile, and the other half into the Zambesi, required but little imagination to originate, seeing the actual visitor would not feel bound to say how the division was effected. He could only know the fact of waters rising at one spot, and separating to flow north and south. The conical tops to the mound look like invention, as also do the names.

'A slave, bought on Lualaba East, came from Lualaba West in about twelve days. These two Lualabas may form the loop depicted by Ptolemy, and Upper and Lower Tanganyika be a third arm of the Nile.'

His ulcerated feet now became worse and worse. He could not plant them on the ground without causing a discharge of bloody matter. In January 1871 he was still detained at Bambarré. He termed the Manyuema people the most callous, bloody savages he ever knew. One puts a scarlet feather from a parrot's tail on the ground, and challenges those near to stick it in the hair. He who does so must kill a man or woman. No one was allowed to wear the skin of the musk cat unless he had murdered somebody. Guns alone, he said, prevented them from killing them all. His men, who had been despatched to the coast, arrived on the 4th February, demanding more money from him, and declaring they had orders from the Consul to force him back. He reached the Lualaba on the 31st March. The part of the river he had reached was 3000 yards across. Although under the impression that it was one of the feeders of the Nile, he suspected it might be the Congo—a conclusion established by Stanley's more recent discovery that it is identical with the river Zaire or Congo. His ink having failed him here, he was driven to the expedient of writing with the juice of a plant across old newspapers. His life was also endangered here by a plot amongst his men, who intended to destroy him. They did all in their power to prevent him crossing the Lualaba. He determined to return to Ujiji for other men. He reached Ujiji on the 23d October, and Mr. H. M. Stanley, leader of Mr. Bennett's Livingstone Search Expedition, arrived on the 28th.

'The great traveller,' says Mr. Stanley, 'was reduced to a skeleton by illness and fatigue; he was sick, destitute, and forlorn. All his men except four had either deserted or had died, and there seemed to be no hope for him. His piteous appeals for help to his friends at Zanzibar were either neglected or his letters were lost. There was no prospect but that of lingering illness and death before him. Under the influence, however, of good cheer and nourishing food, and, perhaps, social fellowship with another of his race, he speedily recovered, and in six or seven days after his rescue was enabled to accompany a portion of the American expedition in a boat to the north end of Lake Tanganyika, where both Livingstone and the author saw a river running through a broad gorge enclosed by lofty mountains into the lake, with no possible outlet whatever at any part in the firmly-connected mountain walls which surround the entire northern hal. of the Tanganyika. After a journey of 750 miles, and a residence of over four months together, Livingstone and the American expedition became parted for ever at Unyanyembé, on 14th March 1872.'

Before parting with Stanley, the following interesting con-versation took place :—

'Doctor,' said Stanley, 'so far as I can understand it, you do not intend to return home until you have satisfied yourself about the "Sources of the Nile." When you have satisfied yourself, you will come home and satisfy others. Is it not so?'

'That is it exactly. When your men come back' (the men whom Stanley was to hire at Zanzibar), 'I shall immediately start for Ufipa' (on the south-eastern shores of Lake Tanganyika); 'then . . . I shall strike south, and round the extremity of Lake Tanganyika. Then a south-east course will take me to Chikumbis, on the Lualaba. On crossing the Lualaba, I shall go direct south-west to the copper mines of Katanga. Eight days south of Katanga the natives declare the fountains to be. When I have found them, I shall return by Katanga to the underground houses of Rua. From the caverns, ten days north-east will take me to Lake Komolendo. I shall be able to travel from the lake in your boat, up the river Lufira, to Lake Lincoln. Then, coming down again, I can proceed north by the Lualaba to the fourth lake, which will, I think, explain the whole problem.'

'And how long do you think this little journey will take you?'

'A year and a half at the farthest from the day I leave Unyanyembé.'

'Suppose you say two years; contingencies might arise, you know. It will be well for me to hire these new men for two years, the day of their engagement to begin from their arrival at Unyanyembé.'

'Yes, that will do excellently well.'

'Now, my dear Doctor, the best of friends must part. You have come far enough; let me beg of you to turn back.'

'Well, I will say this to you, you have done what few men could do—far better than some great travellers I know; and I am grateful to you for what you have done for me. God guide you safe home, and bless you, my friend.'

'And may God bring you safe back to us all, my dear friend. Farewell.'

Livingstone gave a painful enough disclosure of his feelings and circumstances previous to Mr. Stanley's arrival, in a note of thanks to Mr. James Gordon Bennett of the *New York Herald:*—

'If I explain the forlorn condition in which he found me, you will easily perceive that I have good reason to use very strong expressions of gratitude. I came to Ujiji off a tramp of between four and five hundred miles beneath a blazing vertical sun, having been baffled, worried, defeated, and forced to return, when almost in sight of the end of the geographical part of my mission, by a number of half-caste Moslem slaves sent to me from Zanzibar instead of men. The sore heart, made still sorer by the truly woful sights I had seen of "man's inhumanity to man," reacted on the bodily frame, and depressed it beyond measure. I thought that I was dying on my feet. It is not too much to say, that almost every step of

the weary sultry way I was in pain, and I reached Ujiji a
mere ruckle of bones. Here I found that some £500 worth
of goods I had ordered from Zanzibar had unaccountably been
entrusted to a drunken half-caste Moslem tailor, who, after
squandering them for sixteen months on the way to Ujiji,
finished up by selling off all that remained for slaves and ivory
for himself. He had divined on the Koran, and found that I
was dead. He had also written to the governor of Unyanyembé that he had sent slaves after me to Manyuema, who
returned and reported my decease, and begged permission to
sell off the few goods that his drunken appetite had spared.
He, however, knew perfectly well, from men who had seen
me, that I was alive, and waiting for the goods and men; but
as for morality, he is evidently an idiot; and there being no
law here except that of the dagger or musket, I had to sit
down in great weakness, destitute of everything save a few
barter-cloths and beads I had taken the precaution to leave
here in case of extreme need. The near prospect of beggary
among Ujijians made me miserable. I could not despair,
because I laughed so much at a friend who, on reaching the
mouth of the Zambesi, said "that he was tempted to despair
on breaking the photograph of his wife; we could have no
success after that." After that, the idea of despair has to me
such a strong smack of the ludicrous, it is out of the question.

'Well, when I had got to about the lowest verge, vague
rumours of an English visitor reached me. I thought of
myself as the man who went down from Jerusalem to Jericho;
but neither priest, Levite, nor Samaritan could possibly pass
my way. Yet the good Samaritan was close at hand; and one
of my people rushed up at the top of his speed, and in great
excitement gasped out, "An Englishman coming! I see

him!" And off he darted to meet him. An American flag—
the first ever seen in these parts—at the head of a caravan,
told me the nationality of the stranger. I am as cold and
non-demonstrative as we islanders are usually reputed to be,
but your kindness made my frame thrill.. It was indeed over-
whelming; and I said in my soul, "Let the richest blessings
descend from the Highest on you and yours."

'The news Mr. Stanley had to tell me was thrilling: the
mighty political changes on the Continent, the success of the
Atlantic cables, the election of General Grant, and many
topics riveted my attention for days together, and had an
immediate and beneficial effect on my health. I had been
without news from home for years, save what I could glean
from a few *Saturday Reviews* and copies of *Punch* for 1868.
The appetite revived, and in a week I began to feel strong
again. Mr. Stanley brought a most kind and encouraging
despatch from Lord Clarendon, whose loss I sincerely deplore,
—the first I have received from the Foreign Office since
1866,—and information that Her Majesty's Government had
kindly sent £1000 to my aid. Up to his arrival I was not
aware of any pecuniary aid. I came unsalaried, but this want
is now happily repaired; and I am anxious that you and all
my friends should know that, though uncheered by letters, I
have stuck to the task which my friend Sir Roderick Murchison set me with John-Bullish tenacity, believing that all will
come right at last.'

Before the end came, he had resolved to satisfy himself
that the Nile really rose where he supposed. Stanley had
urged him to press on no farther; but Livingstone wrote:—
'My judgment said, "All your friends will wish you to make
a complete work of the exploration of the sources of the Nile

before you retire." My daughter Agnes says: "Much as I wish you to come home, I would rather that you finished your work to your own satisfaction than return merely to gratify me." Rightly and nobly said, my darling Nannie. Vanity whispers loudly, "She is a chip of the old block!" My blessing on her and on all the rest.'

So he went on, reaching Unyanyembé, where he remained waiting for some promised help. The following entry occurs in his journal (1872) :—

'19th March.—Birthday. My Jesus, my King, my Life, my All; I again dedicate my whole self to Thee. Accept me, and grant, O gracious Father, that ere this year is gone I may finish my task. In Jesus' name I ask it. Amen, so let it be.

' DAVID LIVINGSTONE.'

An entry on May 31, 1872, is as follows :—'In reference to this Nile source, I have been kept in perpetual doubt and perplexity. I know too much to be positive. Great Lualaba, or Lualubba, as Manyuema say, may turn out to be the Congo or the Nile, a shorter river after all—the fountains flowing north and south seem in favour of its being the Nile. Great westing is in favour of the Congo. It would be comfortable to be positive like Baker. "Every drop, from the passing shower to the roaring mountain-torrent, must fall into Albert Lake, a giant at its birth." How soothing to be positive !'

These doubts about the Nile sources grew stronger, but they never overcame his confidence. He died in the faith that the Nile rose between 10° and 12° south latitude.

Livingstone's death took place on the 1st of May 1873, at Ilala, in Central Africa. For some time previous he had been very weak. Forcing his feeble strength, however, he pushed on, riding on a donkey. Then he had to be carried on a kitanda or bedstead; but soon after reaching Ilala, he gave up travelling, and his servants erected a hut, in which he lay for a few days, gradually growing weaker; and at last, on the day mentioned, he expired.

In his *Last Journals*, the now familiar death-scene is thus recorded :—' The lad's evident alarm made Susi run to arouse Chuma, Chowperé, Matthew, and Muanyaséré; and the six men went immediately to the hut. Passing inside, they looked towards the bed. Dr. Livingstone was not lying on it, but appeared to be engaged in prayer, and they instinctively drew backwards for an instant. Pointing to him, Majwara said, "When I lay down he was just as he is now, and it is because I find that he does not move that I fear he is dead." They asked the lad how long he had slept. Majwara said he could not tell, but he was sure that it was some considerable time. The men drew nearer. A candle, stuck by its own wax to the top of the box, shed a light sufficient for them to see his form. Dr. Livingstone was kneeling by the side of his bed, his body stretched forward, his head buried in his hands upon the pillow. For a minute they watched him. He did not stir. There was no sound of breathing. Then one of them (Matthew) advanced softly to him, and placed his hands to his cheeks. It was sufficient—life had been extinct some time, and the body was almost cold. Livingstone was dead. His sad-hearted servants raised him tenderly up and laid him full length on the bed, then, carefully covering him, they went out into the damp night air to consult together. It was not long before the cocks crew; and it is from this circumstance, coupled with the fact that Susi spoke to him some time shortly before midnight, that we are able to state with tolerable certainty that he expired early on the 1st of May.'

The fourth Livingstone Search Relief Expedition arrived at Zanzibar in February 1873, commanded by Lieutenant Cameron, Murphy, and Dr. Dillon. It was sent to Africa under the auspices of the Geographical Society. At the end of August 1873, the expedition arrived at Unyanyembé; in the following month Chuma, one of Livingstone's servants, appeared in their midst, informing them that Livingstone's body was but twenty days behind, and was being brought up by his followers. Soon afterwards they appeared with their burden, and continued their march to Zanzibar, which they reached in February 1874. The remains of Livingstone were conveyed by ship to Southampton, thence to London. After a formal examination by Sir William Fergusson, the left arm bone, which had been splintered by a lion's jaw over thirty years before, offered convincing evidence that Livingstone was really dead. The body of Livingstone was borne, on Saturday, 18th April 1874, amidst tokens of profound and universal respect, to its last resting-place in Westminster Abbey.

A memorial tablet, with the following inscription, now marks the spot in Westminster Abbey where the remains of Dr. Livingstone are deposited :—'Brought by faithful hands over land and sea, here rests David Livingstone, missionary, traveller, philanthropist. Born March 19, 1813; died May 1, 1873, at Chitambo's village, Ulala. For thirty years his life was spent in an unwearied effort to evangelize the native races, to explore the undiscovered secrets, to abolish the desolating slave trade of Central Africa, and where, with his last words, he wrote : "All I can add in my solitude is, may Heaven's rich blessing come down on every one—American,

English, or Turk—who will help to heal this open sore of the world."' On each side of the tablet are also the following inscriptions:—'Tantus amor veri, nihil est quod noscere malim, quam fluvii causas per sæcula tanta latentes;' and: 'Other sheep I have which are not of this fold: them also I must bring, and they shall hear my voice.'

A Livingstone memorial statue has been erected in the East Princes Street Gardens, Edinburgh. The statue represents Livingstone in thorough travelling costume; in his right hand a Bible, and a revolver in his belt. The statue stands about eight feet high, and is from the design of Mrs. D. O. Hill. As a further honour, Stanley has suggested that the great Lualaba-Congo river be henceforth known as the 'Livingstone.'

Amongst the tributes to his memory, few are more correct and appropriate than that by Sir Samuel W. Baker:—'The life of Dr. Livingstone is well known; but although his character as an explorer has been established for many years, there are few persons beyond scientific geographers who truly appreciate his enormous labours. When we examine the maps of all his published works, we must be struck with amazement that any one man should have been able to support the bodily fatigue of travelling over the many thousand miles in Africa marked by that thin and wandering line of red which denotes his track. The world knows but little of such fatigues —the toil of body in unhealthy climates, the lack of food, constant exposure to both sun and rain, perpetual anxiety, delays, and passive hostility that wear out the brain with over-taxed patience; hopes deferred, followed by that sickness of heart which is a greater strain upon the nervous system than the heaviest physical work. These are the trials that Livingstone sustained throughout his life of exploration; and still he endured until he dropped upon his road, worn out in his great work; and in solitude he died upon his knees by his bedside, far from the world, but in communion at the last with Him who had been his guide and protector through a life of difficulties and perils.

'His geographical opinions. may or may not be accepted on all points, but there can only be one opinion concerning the man: he was the greatest of all explorers of this century; he was one of a noble army of martyrs who have devoted their lives to the holy cause of freedom; and he has laid down his life as a sacrifice upon a wild and unknown path, upon which he has printed the first footsteps of civilisation.'

RECENT AFRICAN EXPLORATION.

The first 'Livingstone Search Expedition' was despatched by the Royal Geographical Society under Lieutenant Dawson, with the view of carrying food and supplies to Dr. Livingstone. They had only reached Bagamoyo, on the African coast, when a message was received from Mr. Stanley to the effect that he had discovered Livingstone, and that the great traveller objected to any 'slave' expedition being sent to him. Lieutenant Dawson therewith resigned the command of the expedition, which in turn was taken up by Mr. New, who died shortly afterwards; then by Lieutenant Henn, R.N.; and lastly by Mr. Oswell Livingstone, a son of Dr. Livingstone. The latter also gave up the idea of reaching his father, and the expedition was abandoned. When the Geographical Society resolved on utilizing the remainder of their funds in another expedition, Lieutenant Cameron was chosen com-

mander.   He drew up his scheme of exploration by way of
Victoria Nyanza, Mounts Kenia and Kilimanjaro, and the
Albert Nyanza, and thence through Ulegga and Nyangwe
down the Congo to the west coast.   When he had reached
Unyamyembé, two-thirds on the way to Tanganyika, on the
20th October 1873, while lying in bed blind and almost lifeless, the news was brought to him of Livingstone's death.   On
18th February 1874, his eye rested on the blue expanse of
Lake Tanganyika, which had been discovered by Captain
Burton fifteen years previously.   After three years of unheard-
of difficulties, in November 1875 he emerged at Benguela, on
the west coast, to which he had made his way 2000 miles as
the crow flies, from Bagamoyo on the east coast.   Some of the
results of his journey are his exploration of the southern water-
parting of the Congo, and the fixing of the latitude and
longitude of all the places at which he halted.

An expedition sent by the Portuguese Government has been
very successful.   One division, led by Major Pinto, has crossed
Africa in a south-easterly direction from Benguela to Natal,
and made a complete exploration of the Upper Zambesi, and
discovered a navigable river called the Cuando.

Missionary effort is following up the work done by explorers ;
the English Universities Mission is at the northern extremity
of Lake Nyassa ; Livingstonia is the seat of the Scottish Free
Church Mission ; the Established Church of Scotland is at
Blantyre (after the birthplace of Livingstone) ; the London
Missionary Society at Ujiji, Lake Tanganyika ; and the Church
Missionary Society at Lake Victoria Nyanza.   The Church
Mission has also sent representatives to King Mtesa in
Uganda.   The Baptist Mission is making a settlement on the
Congo.

SIR SAMUEL WHITE BAKER, M.A., F.R.G.S.

PART I.

The Albert Nyanza—Great Basin of the Nile—Explorations of the Nile Sources.

THE great African traveller, Sir Samuel Baker, K.C.B., F.R.S., the son of Samuel Baker, Thorngrove, Worcestershire, was born in 1821. Having been educated as an engineer, he showed a desire for travel at an early age, and went to Ceylon, where he was partly occupied, along with his brother Col. Baker, in organizing an agricultural settlement. Fond also of sport and adventure, he published *The Rifle and Hound in Ceylon*, 1854, and *Eight Years' Wanderings in Ceylon*, 1855. He married a young Hungarian lady in 1860, who has since been the companion of many of his wanderings. In March 1861 he formed the resolution to organize an expedition for the discovery of the sources of the Nile, and with the hope of meeting the East African expedition of Captains Speke and Grant, which had been sent from the south by the English Government, by way of Zanzibar, for the same object. From youth upwards he had been inured to hardships and endurance in wild sports in tropical climates; he besides possessed a tough constitution, perfect independence, and the time and means for the accomplishment of the object.

She, 'the dear, near, and true,' with whom his life was linked, his devoted wife, had determined also to accompany him. 'One who, although my greatest comfort,' he writes, 'was also my greatest care; one whose life yet dawned at so early an age that womanhood was still a future. I shuddered at the prospect for her, should she be left alone in savage lands at my death; and gladly would I have left her in the luxuries of home instead of exposing her to the miseries of Africa. It was in vain that I implored her to remain, and that I painted the difficulties and perils still blacker than I supposed they really would be : she was resolved, with woman's constancy and devotion, to share all dangers, and to follow me through each rough footstep of the wild life before me.' So together they sailed up the Nile from Cairo, on the 15th April 1861. Within twenty-six days from Cairo they arrived at Korosko, from whence, starting across the Nubian desert, they reached the river again at Abou Hamed. Berber was the next town which they reached. Resolving to become independent of interpreters as quickly as possible, the plan of exploration for the first year was arranged to embrace the affluents to the Nile from the Abyssinian range of mountains; also to follow up the Atbara river from its junction with the Nile, twenty miles south of Berber; to examine also all the Nile tributaries from the south-east as far as the Blue Nile. Having explored all the Abyssinian affluents of the Nile, Baker descended the Blue Nile to Khartoum.

The waters of the Blue Nile, or Bahr el Azrek, are described as delicious; those of the White Nile are said to be seldom clear, and to have a disagreeable taste of vegetation. The Blue Nile, being a mountain stream, rises and falls with great rapidity; the other is of lake origin, and flows through vast marshes. The Atbara is perfectly dry during some months of the year; but from June to the middle of September the storms are terrific, and every ravine becomes a raging torrent. The river bed is perfectly dry from the beginning of March to June, with pools at intervals of every few miles, in which congregate all the inhabitants of the river — the crocodiles, hippopotami, fish, and large turtle—until the floods again set them at liberty. The rainy season begins in Abyssinia in the middle of May, but, owing to the parched nature of the soil, the torrents do not begin to fill until the middle of June. The Blue Nile and the Atbara receive the entire drainage of Abyssinia, and pour their entire floods into the main Nile in the middle of June; and it is the sudden rush of water descending from Abyssinia which causes the inundation of the Nile in Lower Egypt.

Baker found the town of Khartoum, which is situated on a point of land forming the angle between the White and Blue Niles at their junction, to be a miserable, filthy, and unhealthy spot. All around there is the sandy desert. The town, consisting of about 30,000 inhabitants, is chiefly composed of huts of unburnt brick, is densely crowded, and there are neither drains nor cesspools. The natives consist of Greeks, Syrians, Copts, Armenians, Turks, Arabs, and Egyptians. There are consuls for France, Austria, and America resident in the town. It is the seat of government for the Soudan provinces; about six thousand troops were quartered in the town in 1861. The Egyptian soldier, being badly paid, and under loose discipline, carries out a

system of forage and plunder. The Governor-General of the
Soudan in 1862 was Moosa Pasha, a Turkish official who
shared all the failings of his race. 'Misgovernment, monopoly,
extortion, and oppression are the certain accompaniments of
Turkish administration. At a great distance from all civilisation, and separated from Lower Egypt by the Nubian deserts,
Khartoum affords a wide field for the development of Egyptian
official character. Every official plunders ; the Governor-
General extorts from all sides; he fills his private pockets by
throwing every conceivable obstacle in the way of progress,
and embarrasses every commercial movement in order to
extort bribes from individuals. From the highest to the
lowest official, dishonesty and deceit are the rule, and each
robs in proportion to his grade in the Government employ,
the onus of extortion falling upon the natives ; thus exorbitant
taxes are levied upon the agriculturists, and the industry of
the inhabitants is disheartened by oppression. The taxes are
collected by the soldiery, who naturally extort by violence
an excess of the actual impost ; accordingly, the Arabs limit
their cultivation to their bare necessities.' The slave trade
was then the curse of Soudan, and every one in Khartoum,
with the exception of a few Europeans, was in favour of the
slave trade, the White Nile being the great nursery of
supply.

The Egyptian authorities at Khartoum showed no willing-
ness to assist Baker in organizing an expedition to discover
the Nile sources. They had no wish to encourage English
explorations of the slave-producing districts, as this understood
an exposure of the odious traffic, and probable interference
by the English Government. An application to the British
Consul at Alexandria for a few soldiers and boats to aid him

in this difficult enterprise was refused. At last preparations were made for sailing; the vessels necessary for the voyage to Gondokoro, the navigable limit of the Nile, were secured. An extra quantity of provisions was embarked, in the hope of meeting Speke and Grant's party. In the boats were conveyed twenty-one donkeys, four camels, and four horses, for use afterwards in land transport. A demand for a certain tax for every man on board the boats, made just as they were ready to start, was refused. The voyage up the Nile was comparatively uneventful. A German servant, Johann, who accompanied Baker, and who was engaged at Khartoum while in failing health, died on the voyage southwards. 'Verily, it is a pleasant voyage,' writes Baker, rather sarcastically, on the 2d January 1863; 'disgusting naked savages, everlasting marshes teeming with mosquitoes, and the entire country devoid of anything of either common interest or beauty. Course west the whole day; saw giraffes and one ostrich on the east bank. On the west bank there is a regular line of villages throughout the day's voyage, within half a mile of each other; the country very thickly populated. The huts are of mud, thatched, having a very small entrance; they resemble button mushrooms. The Shillooks are wealthy; immense herds of cattle swarm throughout their country.' At another time he writes: 'The windings of this monotonous river are extraordinary, and, during dead calms in these vast marshes, the feeling of melancholy produced is beyond description.'

The natives of Nuëhr village struck Baker as being something superlative in the way of savages: the men were completely naked; their bodies were rubbed with ashes, and their hair stained red by a plaster of ashes and cow's urine. The chief of the village, with his wife and daughter, paid them a visit, asking for all that they saw in the shape of bracelets, but declining a knife as useless. The women. he thought very ugly. The men were tall and powerful, armed with lances, and carrying pipes which would contain nearly a quarter of a pound of tobacco. They are accustomed to smoke either tobacco or charcoal. The shooting of a fat young hippopotamus was the signal for a cauldron of hippopotamus soup. This led him to remark that 'real turtle is mock hippopotamus.' Arriving at Zareeba, the station of an Austrian White Nile trader, the latter presented them with a bullock. Here they had a sight of the chief of the Kytch tribe, who wore a leopard skin across his shoulders, and a skull-cap of white beads, with a crest of white ostrich feathers. His daughter was a good - looking girl of sixteen, whose only clothing consisted of a little piece of dressed hide, about a foot wide, slung across her shoulders. The entire tribe had a half-starved appearance. So emaciated were they, that they looked as if they had no visible posteriors, and their long thin legs and arms gave them a peculiar gnat-like appearance. They devour both the skins and bones of all dead animals; the bones they pound between stones, and, when these are reduced to powder, they are boiled to a kind of porridge.

On 23d January they arrived at the Austrian mission station of St. Croix, where the missionary, Herr Morlang, acknowledged that the mission was absolutely useless among such savages. Accordingly the whole village and mission station was sold to Koorshid Aga for £30 ! Baker purchased a horse from the missionaries. Herr Morlang described the whole of the White Nile traders as a mere colony of robbers, who pillaged and shot the natives at discretion. On 29th

January they passed a multitude of cattle and natives on the right bank. These natives make tumuli of dung, which being constantly on fire, accumulates; fresh fuel is added to keep the pile burning, and in order to drive away the mosquitoes. The cattle crowd round these piles, living with the natives in the smoke. The heaps of ashes become about eight feet high, when they are used as sleeping-places and watch-stations by the natives, who, rolling themselves amongst the ashes, have a very ghastly appearance.

The 'Shir' tribe they found well armed with ebony clubs, lances, bows and arrows. The women here wear leather aprons, with a strip of leather hanging down behind resembling a tail. The women carry their children in a skin slung from their shoulders across the back, and secured by a thong round the waist. Their huts or dwelling-places are circular, the entrances being so low that the natives creep both in and out upon their hands and knees. The most valuable article of barter for this tribe is the iron hoe. The lotus seed is utilized by all the tribes of the White Nile, the seed being ground into flour, and made into a kind of porridge. On 2d February they arrived safely at Gondokoro.

Gondokoro consists merely of a few miserable grass huts. Formerly it was a mission station. Then it was occupied for about two months of the year only by the ivory traders. The climate is hot and unhealthy, but the place was a great improvement upon the interminable marshes through which they had been passing. The dwellers in Gondokoro are the Bari tribe. The men are described as well-grown; the women are not prepossessing, but are awanting in the negro type of thick lips and flat nose. The features are good. Their skin is tattooed and rubbed with a mixture of ochre and grease, which gives them the appearance of new red bricks. The most deadly weapons they possess are their poisoned arrows. When they enter the system, death is almost certain to follow.

When Baker arrived, he was looked upon by the slave-traders as a spy sent by the British Government. In approaching the encampments of the different traders, the sounds which were heard were the clanking of fetters, as the slaves were being driven to their hiding-places as secretly as possible. Baker's presence was considered as an unwarrantable intrusion, and he was looked upon as a stumbling-block to the trade. The traders' people, to the number of about six hundred, seemed to spend their time in drinking, quarrelling, and ill-treating the slaves. Guns were also being fired off in the most promiscuous and dangerous fashion. Baker's men mutinied while staying here, and to go farther with such faithless servants looked as if the expedition would be a failure. But by the tact of Baker and his wife, order and regularity were restored.

On the 15th February, the sound of musketry was heard at a great distance, and a dropping fire from the south. The report was that ivory porters were coming from the next station, and that two white men were with them who had come from the sea. Baker ran to meet them, in the hope that they might be Speke and Grant. He was correct in his supposition. All his men suddenly became mad with excitement, and firing salutes with ball cartridge, one of the donkeys was shot. 'When I first met them,' writes Baker, 'they were walking along the bank of the river towards my boats. At a distance of about a hundred yards I recognised my old friend Speke, and with a heart beating with joy I took off

my cap and gave a welcome hurrah as I ran towards him.
For the moment he did not recognise me; ten years' growth
of beard and moustache had worked a change; and as I was
totally unexpected, my sudden appearance in the centre of
Africa appeared to him incredible. I hardly required an
introduction to his companion, as we felt already acquainted;
and after the transports of this happy meeting, we walked
together to my diabbiah, my men surrounding us with smoke
and noise by keeping up an unremitting fire of musketry the
whole way. We were shortly seated on deck under the awning,
and such rough fare as could be hastily prepared was set
before these two ragged, careworn specimens of African travel,
whom I looked upon with feelings of pride as my own
countrymen. As a good ship arrives in harbour, battered and
torn by a long and stormy voyage, yet sound in her frame
and seaworthy to the last, so both these gallant travellers
arrived in Gondokoro. Speke appeared the more worn of
the two; he was excessively lean, but in reality he was in
good tough condition; he had walked the whole way from
Zanzibar, never having once ridden during the wearying
march. Grant was in honourable rags, his bare knees pro-
jecting through the remnants of trousers that were an exhibition
of rough industry in tailor's work. He was looking tired and
feverish, but both men had a fire in the eye that showed the
spirit that had led them through.'

Baker thought at first that the mystery of the Nile sources
was completely unravelled, and even said to Speke, 'Does not
one leaf of the laurel remain for me?' It was then made
evident that although Speke and Grant had discovered the
Victoria Nyanza, there was another lake called the Luta
Nzige, which must be a second source of the Nile. It

entered this unknown lake at its northern extremity, while the body of the lake came from the south. Speke wrote in Baker's journal such instructions as he thought might be useful to him, and Grant furnished him with a map of their route and explorations. They parted on 26th February, when Speke and Grant sailed from Gondokoro.

Baker had arranged with Mahommed, an ivory trader, that he and his men should accompany them in their journey southwards. To this he apparently assented, but it was afterwards found that when they were most friendly, they were plotting against him, and had determined to ruin the expedition. Baker, receiving some hints of their intention, took decided steps to arrest the progress of the mutiny; he found, however, that a boy named Saat, and Richarn, an habitual drunkard, were the only two amongst his company who remained faithful to him. Rendered utterly helpless, Baker decided to leave all his baggage in charge of a friendly chief of the Baris at Gondokoro, take two fast dromedaries for his servant Richarn and Saat, two horses for Mrs. Baker and himself, and so make a push through the hostile tribes until he came amongst those who were friendly, and afterwards to trust to fortune. But his friendly servant, arguing with him, showed the danger and impossibility of this method of travel. Seventeen of his old servants were therefore coerced to join the expedition, although an intention to desert on their part, once the journey was begun, was well known to their leader. They took their departure from Gondokoro on the 26th of March 1863. Richarn and Saat were in high spirits when the start was made; Mrs. Baker was mounted on an old Abyssinian hunter ' Tetel,' Baker rode ' Filfil,' and the camels and donkeys were all heavily loaded. They had neither guide nor interpreter, the natives being too much under the influence of the traders to volunteer their services.

The first halt was made at Belignan, where they overtook the traders' party which had been so unfriendly to them at Gondokoro. Two men, deserting from their company, promised to act as guides and interpreters for ninety miles forward. Pushing on through ravine and jungle, it was plain that the camels were overloaded; the donkeys proved themselves better suited for the roughness and inequalities of the road. Within six miles of Ellyria, Baker riding in front along with his wife, they were met by five or six hundred natives, who pressed around them. A humpback interpreter put them through the following cross-examination. It may be explained that Mrs. Baker was dressed in similar fashion to her husband, in a pair of loose trousers and gaiters, with a blouse and belt, the only difference being that she wore long sleeves, while her husband went with his arms uncovered. 'In reply,' writes Baker, 'to a question to the humpback, he asked me who I was. I explained that I was a traveller. "You want ivory?" he said. "No," I answered, "it is of no use to me." "Ah, you want slaves?" he replied. "Neither do I want slaves," I answered. This was followed by a burst of laughter from the crowd, and the humpback continued his examination. "Have you got plenty of cows?" "Not one; but plenty of beads and copper." "Plenty! where are they?" "Not far off; they will be here presently with my men," and I pointed to the direction from which they would arrive. "What countryman are you?" "An Englishman." He had never heard of such people. "You are a Turk?" "All right," I replied; "I am anything you like." "And that is your son?" (pointing at Mrs. Baker). "No, she is my wife."

" Your wife ! What a lie ! He is a boy." "Not a bit of
it," I replied; "she is my wife, who has come with me to
see the women of this country." "What a lie !" he again
politely rejoined.'

The antics of a 'Wallady,' a monkey, diverted the natives
very much, though he seemed to have an antipathy to black
people. He was remarkably fond of Mrs. Baker, and seemed
uneasy out of her sight. Arrived in the country of Ellyria,
they were fortunate enough to make friendship with the
trader's party formerly hostile to them. The chief Legge
proved himself to be a greedy, brutal, and ignorant savage,
who made the most of the travellers, but who would give
nothing in return. He swallowed a pint bottle of the strongest
spirits of wine which had been offered to him, allowing it to
trickle down his throat like water, and afterwards asked for
more. Baker sketched the face of this remarkable chief for
his portfolio. ' Of all the villainous countenances that I have
ever seen,' he says, ' that of Legge excelled.'

Leaving the valley of Ellyria, in crossing the flat country
beyond they had an opportunity of observing the marching
order of the trader's party. ' Several of the people were
mounted on donkeys, some on oxen; the most were on
foot, including all the women to the number of about sixty,
who were the slaves of the trader's people. These carried
heavy loads; and many in addition to the burdens carried
children strapped to their backs in leather slings.' These
women were forced along by their brutal owners, and frequently beaten to urge their progress. The flag, guarded by
eight or ten men, leads the trader's party; a native, carrying
a box of five hundred cartridges in case of attack, walks
beside them. In single file the porters and baggage follow,

with soldiers at intervals to guard in case of runaways. The ammunition was carried by about fifteen natives in the centre. Another flag was carried in the rear of the party, and behind this no straggler is allowed. Crossing the Kanieti river, a tributary of the Sobat, and the latter again of the Nile, they arrived at the village of Wakkala. The village consisted of about seven hundred houses, strongly protected by a system of palisades made of 'babanoose,' the hard iron-wood of the country. A hedge of thorns strengthened this fence. Since leaving Gondokoro, game had been extremely scarce; but in the neighbourhood of this village there was abundance. Here they tasted meat for the first time since leaving the latter place. Another halt was made in the neighbourhood of Latomi, one of the principal places in the Latooka country. Here Baker's men carried out their former threat, and attempted to mutiny. The ringleaders having been dealt with in rather a summary manner, order was again restored. An incident occurred on the march which elevated Baker in the eyes of the leader of the party, and also of the Turks themselves. One of the native porters suddenly throwing down his load made off at full speed, pursued by half-a-dozen Turks, who shouted, ' Shoot him ! shoot him !' ' Knock him over.' Baker gave chase after him on his horse ' Filfil,' and speedily overtook him. But for his interposition, he would have been shot, or well lashed; as it was, he took his burden and joined the others as if nothing had happened. Thus it was that the Turks now regarded him as an ally, and the Latookas as their friend, in having saved their comrade.

On arriving at Tarrangollé, one of the chief towns of Latooka, the natives crowded around to witness the two objects of great interest to them—the camels, and a white woman. These Latookas are remarkably fine savages; their average height is 5 ft. 11½ in., and they possess a splendid muscular development, their arms and legs being beautifully proportioned. The appearance of their countenances is rather pleasing, as they have high foreheads, large eyes, high cheek-bones, mouths not very large, well shaped, and the lips rather full. Our travellers found them frank and warlike, not morose, but ready for either a laugh or a fight. The town of Tarrangollé comprised about three thousand houses; every house was fortified by a little stockaded courtyard, and the town itself was surrounded by iron-wood palisades. The wealth of the Latookas consists for the most part in their cattle, which are most carefully kept. The houses are usually bell-shaped, others are like a candle extinguisher; the roofs are neatly thatched, the roof forming a cap which descends to within two feet and a half of the ground. The doorway is only two feet and two inches high; the interior is entirely dark, as neither here nor elsewhere have they risen to the idea of having windows. The bodies of these savages are entirely nude. The greatest attention is paid to their head-dress. To perfect their *coiffure* requires a period of from eight to ten years. 'The Latookas,' writes Baker, 'wear most exquisite helmets, all of which are formed of their own hair, and are, of course, fixtures. . . . The thick, crisp wool is woven with fine twine, formed from the bark of a tree, until it presents a thick net-work of felt. As the hair grows through this matted substance, it is subjected to the same process, until, in the course of years, a compact substance is formed like a strong felt, about an inch and a half thick, that has been trained into the shape of a helmet. A strong rim, of about two inches deep, is formed by sewing it together with thread; and the front part of the helmet is protected by a piece of polished copper, while a piece of the same metal, shaped like the half of a bishop's mitre, and about a foot in length, forms the crest.' These elaborate head-dresses are occasionally ornamented with shells or beads, according to the taste of the owner.

Their fighting weapons consist of the lance, a powerful iron-headed mace, a long-bladed knife or sword, and an iron bracelet, armed with knife-blades about four inches long by half an inch broad; their shields are made of either buffalo's hide or of giraffe's.

The women are exceedingly plain in their personal appearance. They wear long tails like those of horses, and aprons of tanned leather. Bokké, the wife of the chief, and her daughter, were the only pretty women he saw in the country. Baker had an interview with this chief of Latooka; his wife and daughter also visited him, and they were loaded with presents. Bokké suggested that Mrs. Baker would be much improved if she would extract her four front teeth from the lower jaw, according to the fashion of the country; also that she should pierce her under lip, and wear the long, pointed, polished crystal, about the size of a drawing pencil, which is generally worn by the women of the Latookas. Women are mere servants; they grind the corn, fetch the water, gather firewood, cement the floors, and cook the food. The price of a strong, good-looking young woman would be ten cows. A family of daughters in Latooka is thus exceedingly profitable. 'The simple rule of proportion,' writes Baker, 'will suggest that if one daughter is worth ten cows, ten daughters must be worth a hundred, therefore a large family is the source of wealth; the girls produce the cows, and the boys milk them. All being perfectly naked (I mean the girls and the boys), there is no expense, and the children act as herdsmen to the flocks as in patriarchal times. A multiplicity of wives thus increases wealth by the increase of family. I am afraid this practical state of affairs will be a strong barrier to missionary enterprise. A savage holds to his cows and his women, but especially to his cows.'

While staying at Latooka, they heard that a party of Turks, in attacking a village on the mountains for plunder or slaves, had been exterminated. The attacking party consisted of 110 armed men, in addition to 300 natives. They succeeded in burning a village and in capturing a great number of slaves. These slaves had afterwards retaliated, forced the aggressors to retreat, and had driven them over a precipice. The brutality of the trader's party, shown towards the natives of Latooka, nearly brought about a war. It was only averted when the natives discovered that they must have been hopelessly beaten.

A proposal made by Adda, a chief, led Baker to moralize on the obtuseness of the nature of the savage. He asked him to join him in attacking a village to procure hoes. 'Come along with me,' he said; 'bring your men and guns, and we will attack a village near here, and take their molotes (hoes) and cattle; you keep the cattle, and I will have the molotes.' On being asked whether the village was in an enemy's country, he continued, 'Oh, no! it is close here; but the people are rather rebellious, and it will do them good to kill a few, and to take their molotes. If you are afraid, never mind, I will ask the Turks to do it.' Adda concluded that it must be weakness which caused such conduct. Baker's feelings at the time were noted in his journal:—'1863, 10th April, Latooka.—I wish the black sympathizers in England could see Africa's inmost heart as I do; much of their sympathy would subside. Human nature viewed in its crude state as pictured amongst African savages is quite on a level with that of the brute, and not to be compared with the noble character of the dog. There is neither gratitude, pity, love, nor self-denial; no idea of duty; no religion; but covetousness, ingratitude, selfishness, and cruelty. All are thieves, idle, envious, and ready to plunder and enslave their weaker neighbours.' This is certainly a dark picture, and there is all too good ground for admitting its truthfulness. At the same time, Mungo Park and that greatest of missionary travellers, David Livingstone, both wandered among the heathens of Africa, and discovered the existence of virtues which had not been dreamt of before. The same may be said of the explorations of Mr. H. M. Stanley, whose passage across the 'Dark Continent' had so provoked the hostility of the natives. When at their best, as in the case of King Mtesa of Uganda, or King Rumanika, they presented many virtues which only required patient Christian training and less untoward surroundings to develop into useful and presentable types of manhood.

The curious custom of the funeral dance led Baker to question an intelligent chief called Commoro regarding this musical festivity in honour of the dead, also the habit of exhuming and scattering abroad the bones of those who had long been buried. He had no better reason to give than that it had been the custom of his forefathers. The idea of existence after death was perfectly unthinkable for him.

Commoro: 'Existence *after* death! How can that be? Can a dead man get out of his grave, unless we dig him out?'

'Do you think man is like a beast, that dies and is ended?'

Commoro : 'Certainly. An ox is stronger than a man ; but he dies, and his bones last longer ; they are bigger. A man's bones break quickly; he is weak.'

'Is not a man superior in sense to an ox? Has he not a mind to direct his actions?'

Commoro : 'Some men are not so clever as an ox. Men must sow corn to obtain food, but the ox and wild animals can procure it without sowing.'

And so the discussion proceeded, it seeming impossible the while to impress his mind with anything beyond the seen and temporal. Baker, in explaining the object of his visit to the country, did not succeed any better; for Commoro said, 'Suppose you get to the great lake, what will you do with it? What will be the good of it? If you find that the large river does flow from it, what then? What's the good of it?' Baker in turn explained that England had an intimate knowledge of the whole world except the interior of Africa, and that the object in exploring was to benefit the unknown countries in introducing legitimate trade and commerce. Commoro replied that the Turks would never trade fairly, that they were extremely bad people, and that the only way in which they would purchase ivory was by bartering cattle, which they stole from one tribe in order to sell to another.

One of the amusements of Latooka was elephant-hunting, in which Baker excelled, although on one occasion it was at the risk of his life, being pursued by a large bull-elephant while riding an exhausted horse. The traders' party found Baker's camp exceedingly useful to them, being supplied with many articles which they needed ; they did not scruple to send daily for what they required. Having attained celebrity as a gunsmith, hardly a day passed but what some broken guns were brought to him for repair. Baker and Ibrahim, the chief of the Turks' party, received presents from the natives of Obbo, a town south-west from Latooka. As the people were friendly, Ibrahim determined to pay them a visit; and Baker, delighted to change the scene of his present inaction, started with them on 2d May 1863. Five men were left in charge of Baker's camp and its effects, while the chief Commoro promised to see after its safety. The chief of Obbo, he remarks, might have been the clown of a pantomime, and was far from preserving the dignity of his office, but gave them a very kindly reception, however. The return march furnished the excitement of a giraffe hunt. Sickness now spread among the animals; five donkeys died within a few days, while the remainder looked poor. The Latookas at once ate these animals. Two of the camels died suddenly, having eaten of a poison bush. Mrs. Baker had an attack of gastric fever, and the small-pox had broken out amongst the Turks.

The first clue to the lake Albert Nyanza was received from Wani, the guide and interpreter. He stated that Magungo was situated on a lake so large that no one knew its limits. Large vessels arrived at Magungo from distant parts, bringing cowrie shells and beads in exchange for ivory. After a long stay amongst the Latookas, a start was made for the Obbo country on 23d June 1863, although Mrs. Baker was at the time dangerously ill with bilious fever. The traders' party with whom they journeyed had provoked the hostility of the Latookas, making it dangerous to remain amongst them. Without the presence of this party, also, he would have been unable to procure porters. Arrived at his former hut in the Obbo country, he found that a great change had taken place.

Old Katchiba, the chief, on meeting them, brought them nothing, but said the Turks had eaten up the country. They had indeed arrived in a land of starvation. The natives refused to supply provisions for beads; they would barter nothing save in exchange for flesh. At first they had nothing to eat except tullaboon, a small bitter grain used instead of corn by the natives. In bad health and ill humour, Baker wrote thus in his journal:—'I hear that the Turks intend to make a razzia on the Shoggo country near Farajoke; thus they will stir up a wasp's nest for me wherever I go, and render it impossible for my small party to proceed alone, or even to remain in peace. I shall be truly thankful to quit this abominable land; in my experience I never saw such scoundrels as Africa produces, the natives of the Soudan being worse than all. It is impossible to make a servant of any of these people; the apathy, indolence, dishonesty, combined with dirtiness, are beyond description; and their abhorrence of anything like order increases their natural dislike to Europeans. I have not one man even approaching to a servant; the animals are neglected, therefore they die. And were I to die, they would rejoice, as they would immediately join Koorshid's people in cattle-stealing and slave-hunting— charming followers in the time of danger! Such men destroy all pleasure, and render exploration a mere toil.' Baker and his wife were both down with bilious fever; the flies were killing the donkeys. They were tormented with flies by day, with rats and innumerable bugs by night, heavy dew, daily rain, and impenetrable reeking grass, so that the place was rendered about as disagreeable a prison as could exist. On 23d August the last camel died, and only eight donkeys remained out of twenty-one. All the horses and camels were now dead; the damp food caused by the excessive rain was supposed to have hastened this catastrophe.

Accompanied by his wife, he visited the chief Katchiba on 30th August, by whom they were very politely received. The circular hut which he inhabited was about twenty-five feet in diameter, with a narrow doorway obliging the visitor to enter on all-fours. He treated them to a wild, plaintive air on a native harp, to which he sang. Afterwards he sent on a sheep to their hut as a present. In return, he received a gorgeous necklace of valuable beads, which delighted him very much.

The weary months dragged on at Obbo. Worn-down by fever, the prospect of continuing the journey was anything but hopeful. Mrs. Baker fortunately did not suffer quite so much as her husband. All the animals being dead, the remainder of the journey must be performed on foot; and as travelling on foot would have been impossible in their present weak condition, three oxen were purchased and trained in lieu of horses. These oxen were named respectively, 'Beef,' 'Steaks,' and 'Suet.' 'Beef,' who was at first a fine animal, got so bitten with the flies, and so down in condition, that its name was changed to 'Bones.' Baker succeeded in killing a large bull-elephant in the neighbourhood of Obbo, which gratified the natives very much. The start was made at last on 5th January. The march was now through beautiful park-like scenery, very different from the rank and superabundant vegetation of Obbo. Farajoke was the first village at which they arrived. The next halting-place was at the Asua river. Here the Turks made a raid on a native village, bringing with them about three hundred head of cattle, and a number of slaves tied by the neck with a long leathern thong, so as to form a living chain. Shooa was the next halting-place.

Fowls, butter, and goats were here to be had in abundance; and as beads were of great value, the women flocked to Mrs. Baker, bringing presents of milk and flour in exchange for them. The country was pretty well cultivated, large quantities of sesamé being grown and carefully harvested. Two days after their arrival at Shooa, all the Obbo porters absconded. The reason for this disappearance was, that they had heard the expedition was bound for Kamrasi's country. Kamrasi they feared and dreaded. Ibrahim, the chief of the traders' expedition, had done so badly in the way of collecting ivory, that on being guaranteed 100 cantars (10,000 lbs.) of ivory, he agreed to push on to Kamrasi. In improved health, they left Shooa on the 18th January 1864. A march of eight miles brought them to the village of Fatiko, situated upon a plateau of rock upon elevated ground. Here the natives caused the white travellers to undergo a rather painful method of salutation, that of seizing both the hands and raising the arms three times to their full stretch above the head. After about one hundred Fatikos had been introduced, our travellers thought it was time to get out of their way before the other half of the village should have time to operate upon them.

Marching to the Victoria White Nile, they halted at Atada, where there was a ferry. A messenger was sent to King Kamrasi, informing him who they were, when they must certainly await his return. In the meantime, to quicken matters and restore confidence, their presents were displayed, consisting of a handsome Persian carpet about fifteen feet square, and a heap of superb necklaces. At last, after considerable delay, the natives consented to ferry across Mrs. Baker and himself, with Ibrahim, Richarn, and Saat. They were welcomed to a blazing fire, and received something to eat, when Baker endeavoured to lull their suspicions. Traces of Speke's visit were apparent, as a man showed a small string of blue beads which he had received for ferrying him across the river.

The natives of Unyoro exhibited here more decency in clothing than the naked savages amongst whom they had been travelling farther northwards. The women were neatly dressed in short petticoats with a double skirt; many exposed the bosom, while others wore a piece of bark cloth arranged as a plaid across the chest and shoulders. This cloth is produced from the bark of a species of fig tree, the best quality of which is as soft to the touch as woven cotton. Their native blacksmiths were very clever, using iron hammers instead of stone, and drawing fine wire from the thick copper and brass wire which they received from Zanzibar. These natives also make a fine quality of jet-black earthenware, making tobacco-pipes finely worked in imitation of the small egg-shaped gourd. Mrs. Baker's blonde hair was a great wonder to the natives : she was literally mobbed by them to see the extraordinary sight, when caught dressing it in the doorway of her hut. The native huts are large (about 20 feet in diameter), made entirely of reeds and straw, and in the shape of a beehive,—'very different,' as Baker remarks, 'to the dog-kennels of the northern tribes.' They are extremely neat in all that they do ; what they sell is carefully wrapped up in neat parcels, usually formed of the bark of the plantain. They are in the habit of preparing goat-skins, making them as soft as chamois leather. These they cut into squares, and sew together into mantles as neatly as could be done by a European tailor. Beads, while a marketable commodity, owing to their imperishable nature might slacken in demand ; but articles of clothing might here form the basis of a legitimate trade.

Kamrasi treated Baker to an interview, after a most harassing delay, near M'rooli, his capital. He was so weak and ill that he had to be laid on a mat at the king's feet. Kamrasi was a fine-looking man, with prominent eyes, about six feet high, beautifully clean, and dressed in a robe of bark-cloth. His complexion was a dark brown; and he sat on a copper stool placed upon a carpet of leopard skins, and was surrounded by ten of his principal chiefs. Baker's presents were very handsome: a large white Cashmere mantle, a red silk netted sash, a pair of scarlet Turkish shoes, several pairs of socks, a double-barrelled gun and ammunition, and a quantity of first-class beads. The firing of a gun caused some of the crowd to tumble over one another like rabbits, much to the amusement of the king. Baker received as a present, seventeen cows, twenty pots of sour plantain cider, and several loads of unripe plantains. Having heard that the lake was so far distant, all his porters deserted him on 16th February.

Before leaving for the lake, the king showed the genuine greed of his nature by demanding more presents, concluding by the following, expressed in the coolest possible manner: 'I will send you to the lake and to Shooa, as I have promised; but you must leave your wife with me.' The insolence of this last demand drew down upon him the wrath of both Mr. and Mrs. Baker, when in reply he said, in apparent astonishment: 'Don't be angry! I had no intention of offending you by asking for your wife. I will give you a wife, if you want one; and I thought you might have no objections to give me yours —it is my custom to give my visitors pretty wives, and I thought you might exchange. Don't make a fuss about it. If you don't like it, there's an end of it; I will never mention it again.'

Glad to turn his back upon M'rooli, Baker continued his march towards the great lake. The escort provided by Kamrasi was anything but an agreeable one. Crossing the marshes near Kafoor river, Mrs. Baker received a sunstroke, when her life was despaired of. On the frontier of Uganda, worn out with fever and marching and anxiety on account of his wife, whose death was hourly expected, he sank helpless. Mrs. Baker had endured seven days of brain fever, when she recovered in an almost miraculous manner. The moment when this change was observed by the worn-out and anxious explorer is best given in his own words :—'I had slept; and horrified as the idea flashed upon me that she must be dead, and that I had not been with her, I started up. She lay upon her bed, pale as marble, and with that calm serenity that the features assume when the cares of life no longer act upon the mind, and the body rests in death. The dreadful thought bowed me down; but as I gazed upon her in fear, her chest gently heaved, not with the convulsive throbs of fever, but naturally. She was asleep; and when, at a sudden noise, she opened her eyes, they were calm and clear. She was saved! When not a ray of hope remained, God alone knows what helped us. The gratitude of that moment I will not attempt to describe.'

Halting at Parkani, the next stage, it was reported, would bring them to the M'wooten N'zige. That night was a restless one with the explorer, as the goal of his hopes was within reach. Next day, the 14th March, they were early astir, and, pushing forward, reached the summit of a slope from which a good view could be obtained. 'The glory of our prize,' writes Baker, 'burst suddenly upon me! There, like a sea of quicksilver, lay far beneath the grand expanse of water,

—a boundless sea-horizon on the south and south-west, glittering in the noonday sun; and on the west, at fifty or sixty miles' distance, blue mountains rose from the bosom of the lake to a height of about 7000 feet above its level.' As an imperishable memorial of the consort of the Queen, the much-loved Prince Albert, it was named 'The Albert Nyanza.' The beach was perfectly clean sand, the waves throwing up sea-weed as the sea does on an English sea-shore. The lake was known to extend as far south as Karagwé. The eastern shores of the lake, from north to south, were occupied by Chopi, Unyoro, Uganda, Utumbi, and Karagwé. The chief assured them that large canoes had been known to cross over from the other side, but that this required four days and nights of hard rowing to accomplish. Besides, the canoes of Unyoro were not adapted for such a journey. A feast was given to the men in honour of the discovery.

It was with a hopeful and exultant feeling that Baker stood on the shores of the great lake after three years of arduous toil, his pale and exhausted wife, the attendant of his wanderings, beside him. They settled meanwhile in a miserable fishing village near the lake, called Vacovia. The principal product of the country was salt, with which the ground was strongly impregnated. Further examination showed that the lake was a vast depression, far below the general level of the country, surrounded by precipitous cliffs, bounded on the west and south-west by great ranges of mountains from five to seven thousand feet high. The Victoria Nyanza discovered by Speke was a reservoir for the waters of the Nile, formed at a high altitude. The Albert lake, extending much farther north than the Victoria, receives its waters from the latter lake, and forms the grand reservoir for the waters of the Nile. Different affluents were also seen by telescope flowing into the Albert lake from the mountains on the west side.

It was imperatively necessary that what was intended to be accomplished in the way of further exploration should be done at once, as the return to England that year depended upon their being forward at Gondokoro before the end of April. Their guide was sent overland with the oxen to Magungo, where the Victoria Nile emptied its waters into the Albert Nyanza. Boats were ordered for the exploration of the coast northwards from Vacovia to Magungo. Before starting, the whole party were down with fever, which augured ill for the success of the expedition. Eight days were passed at Vacovia before the canoes arrived. They were merely single trees neatly hollowed out, the largest being thirty-two feet long; the one selected for himself was twenty-six feet long, but wider and deeper than the other. On the latter he constructed a framework, thatched with hides, beneath which Mrs. Baker could be defended from the sun and rain. The first part of the voyage was completely successful; before they had reached their destination, however, they had experienced many vicissitudes. Their boatmen deserted, and they made a narrow escape from being upset in a storm on the lake. Several fine herds of elephants were seen in the course of the voyage, bathing together in the lake. Mrs. Baker suffered severely during the voyage: during the day they were cramped in the small cabin, and during the night it invariably rained. The mosquitoes, too, were very troublesome. Arrived at Magungo, the riding oxen were reported to be in good order. They found the fishing arrangements of the natives to be on a most extensive scale. A regular system of basket traps existed along the shores of the lake for the capture of the fish. The portion of a splendid fish, the baggera, was found in the lake; it weighed about fifty pounds. It had evidently been bitten by a crocodile. There are several varieties of fish in the lake which exceed two hundred pounds in weight.

The appearance of the outlet of the lake northwards, looking from Magungo, is thus described by Baker:—'A few miles north there appeared to be a gap in the range, and the lake continued to the west, but much contracted, while the mountain range on the northern side of the gap continued to the north-east. Due north and north-east the country was a dead flat, and far as the eye could reach was an extent of bright green reeds, marking the course of the Nile as it made its exit from the lake. The sheet of water at Magungo, being about seventeen miles in width, ended in a long strip or tail to the north, until it was lost in the flat valley of green rushes. This valley may have been from four to six miles wide, and was bounded upon its west bank by the continuation of the chain of mountains that had formed the western boundary of the lake.' The natives reported that canoes could navigate the Nile in its course from the lake to the Maudi country, as there were no cataracts for a great distance, but both the Maudi and Koslie tribes were reported to be hostile. The current of the river was also said to be so strong that a canoe could not return without many rowers.

In order to prove that the body of dead water which entered the lake at Magungo was really the Victoria Nile, they sailed up the river for eighteen miles, when a gentle current towards the lake became perceptible. The current increased as they proceeded, until they came within sight of a magnificent waterfall. The cliffs on either side were beautifully wooded, rising abruptly to a height of about 300 feet. The river was here contracted into a narrow gorge of scarcely fifty yards in width, and rushing through the gap cleft in the rock, and roaring furiously, it plunged downwards to a depth of 120 feet. In honour of the president of the Royal Geographical Society, Baker named this magnificent cataract the Murchison Falls. They did not succeed, owing to the strength of the current, in bringing their canoes nearer than about 300 yards of the base. A sandbank to their left was literally covered with crocodiles, lying like trunks of trees ready for shipment. After sketching the Murchison Falls, they drifted rapidly downward to the deserted fishing-village whence they had started.

They started as soon as possible on the return journey, their route being parallel with the Victoria Nile. A halt was made at an island in the river called Patooan; but by this time Mr. and Mrs. Baker were both down with fever. The work of exploration was completed, but they had many difficulties to face. Kamrasi, the king of Unyoro, was at war with a neighbouring tribe. The boats which they depended upon for a return to civilisation would certainly have left Gondokoro before they could possibly reach them. Porters could not now be procured at any price to convey their goods from Patooan. Only one riding ox remained alive, and that, too, was half dead. Baker offered the natives all the beads he had (about fifty pounds) and all his baggage, if they would but carry him direct to Shooa from the spot. They were in the midst, too, of the rainy season; neither of them could walk a quarter of a mile without fainting.

They had no guide, and the country was covered with grass and vegetation about eight feet high. Provisions were also scarce, and many of the men connected with the expedition were weak, the whole party having suffered from fever. In his own words, they 'were completely helpless.' Leaving the island of Patooan, as they were determined to proceed, the natives deposited them in a deserted village, half of which was burnt. The hut which they occupied was filthy in the extreme, and flooded with the rain. Here the natives deserted them. 'Every man had absconded,' writes Baker; 'there were neither inhabitants nor provisions; the whole country was a wilderness of rank grass that hemmed us in on all sides; not an animal, nor even a bird, was to be seen; it was a miserable, damp, lifeless country.' Their distress was a little relieved by discovering amongst the ruins of the village some of the seed called 'tullaboon.' So for many a day the daily dinner consisted of a mess of black porridge made from this mouldy seed, with the addition of several vegetables, which were used instead of spinach. A species of wild thyme found in the jungles was used as a substitute for tea. This poor fare, and the effects of the climate, prostrated both Mr. and Mrs. Baker for nearly two months. Baker's vision of perfect happiness at this time was an English beefsteak and a bottle of pale ale, could such have been procured. While the men seemed to thrive on such poor fare, both Mr. and Mrs. Baker were reduced to skeletons. In case of death, Baker wrote instructions in his journal, telling his headman to be sure to deliver his maps, observations, and papers to the English Consul at Khartoum.

Baker now discovered that they were cruelly deserted and were being starved with the knowledge of Kamrasi, king of

Unyoro, his aim being that his men should assist him against the enemy. After two months of suffering at this spot, called Shooa Moru, Baker sent messengers to Kamrasi, who were to explain that he was insulted in treating through a third party in proposing an alliance, that he was a more powerful chief than Kamrasi, and that if he wished his alliance he must treat with him in person. Some days elapsed, when a messenger arrived from Kamrasi with orders that Baker's whole party were to proceed to Kamrasi. On reaching his camp, a meeting took place between Ibrahim, the chief of the Turkish traders, with whom they had formerly journeyed from Gondokoro. The report had previously reached them that both Mr. and Mrs. Baker were dead. The greeting between Baker's party and that of the Turks was very hearty. They all came to kiss Baker's hand and that of his wife, saying, ' By Allah, no woman in the world had a heart so tough as to dare to face what she had gone through.' ' Thank God—be grateful to God.' With the addition of the Turks' party, they now numbered twenty-four armed men.

Baker was not long in discovering, after his arrival at Kisoona, that he had been deceived in his former interview with the king at Atada. Instead of seeing the real king, he had only interviewed his brother. This conduct was the result of pure cowardice and want of faith in Baker's intentions. When Speke passed through the country, he had also been kept waiting for fifteen days before the king had condescended to see him. On the morning after his arrival, the brother of the king called, requesting him to go and visit his royal highness. Baker very pertinently replied that he was hungry and weak from want of food, and that he wanted meat, and not the man who had starved him. A beautiful cow or calf, a fat sheep, and two pots of plantain cider were sent in the afternoon as a present from Kamrasi. The latter, however, kept up his character as a notorious beggar, by sending in the evening for the little double rifle which he always carried, also for his watch and compass. These were refused, and the reason was given that he had failed in his promise to forward him to Shooa ; that he required no presents from him, as he always expected a thousand-fold in return. When the actual introduction to the real Kamrasi took place, Baker threw off the rags in which he had been travelling, and attired himself in a suit of Athole tartan. The king was sitting in a porch in front of a hut, and when Baker approached, he scarcely condescended to look on him, but turned to his attendants and made some remark, which evidently amused them. His brother M'gambi, who had formerly acted the part of the king at M'rooli, sat upon the ground a few feet from Kamrasi. Several of the chiefs sat upon the straw with which the porch was littered. One of his questions was why he had not been to see him before. Baker replied that he had been starved in his country and had not been able.

Concluding that Kisoona would have to be his home until an opportunity occurred for quitting the country for Shooa, Baker constructed a comfortable little hut for his own use, surrounded by a courtyard strongly fenced ; in the latter he arranged an open shed in which to sit during the heat of the day. With plenty of milk, butcher-meat, and flour, the whole party began to look thriving and fat. The natives there never use their milk until it is curdled. The young girls intended as wives of the king are not appreciated unless extremely fat. At an early age, they are forced to swallow about a gallon of curdled milk daily, which has the effect upon them of making them extremely fat. The staple article of food throughout Unyoro is the plantain, which is eaten in several ways. The green plantains are used as potatoes; they are also peeled, cut into thin slices, and dried in the sun. In this state they are stored up, when they are afterwards made into soup. They are also ground into flour; the bark serves as brown paper, and is waterproof. The fibre supplies both thread and cord. The natives proved themselves remarkably sharp at making bargains, and in their dealings required pretty close watching.

It was one day reported that the king intended to pay a visit to the hut of the traveller, and knowing his begging propensities, although little was left of his original baggage except the guns, ammunition, and astronomical instruments, yet everything of any value was hid underneath the beds, in case he should discover that he was in want of something. Kamrasi came with his numerous attendants, but he was scarcely seated in a rude arm-chair, which had been constructed by one of the men, when he asked the chair as a present. The promise was given that one would be made for him immediately. His eye wandering over the hut in search of something which he could ask, and seeing the interior so bare, he laughingly turned to one of his people and said: 'How was it that they wanted so many porters if they have nothing to carry?' A selection of beads having been presented to him, he renewed his request for a No. 24 double rifle, which was refused. Wishing to see the contents of some of the baskets and bags containing several miscellaneous articles, nothing took his fancy except the needles, thread, lancets, medicines, and a small-tooth comb. With the latter article he scratched his own head, when it was handed round amongst the chiefs for a like purpose. The lancets, medicines, and a concave mirror were also examined. After some conversation with the king as to his ancestors, Kamrasi endeavoured to get Baker to acquiesce in a scheme for shooting a chief who was at war with him. Baker declined, telling him plainly that 'he did not intend to mix himself up with his quarrels, that he would harm no one except in self-defence, and that thus he could not be the aggressor. Should the chiefs who were hostile to him, however, Fowooka and Rionga, attack his position, he would be glad to give his aid to repel them. The king left suddenly as if he had been affronted.

Kamrasi was suddenly alarmed while at Kisoona by the report that a hostile trading party had entered his territory, and was marching against him with the intention of attacking the country and killing himself. The king, who was panic-stricken and determined on flight, secured the intervention of Baker, who had the English ensign hoisted on a tall flag-staff in the courtyard. A deputation from the traders' party waited upon Baker, when he assumed high ground in argument, asking them how they dared presume to attack a country under the protection of the British flag; that Unyoro belonged to him by right of discovery, and that he had given the exclusive right to the produce of the country to Ibrahim, the head of the traders' party which had formerly accompanied him southward. He also explained that he would resist any attack that should be made on Kamrasi, and that he would report the whole affair to the Turkish authorities at Khartoum. This had the desired effect, and Kamrasi was freed from the invaders. His first emotions of thankfulness were expressed in a desire to secure the British flag which had worked such wonders. On being refused, he replied : ' If you cannot give me the flag, give me at least that little double-barrelled rifle that you do not require, as you are going home ; then I can defend myself should the Turks attack me.' This rifle was refused, now for about the twentieth time.

Drums were beaten, horns were blown, and singing and dancing took place in all directions when it was known on the following day that the hostile traders' party had retreated across the Nile, as agreed upon. A reply reached Baker from Mahommed Wat-el-Mek, the leader of the party, saying that he was neither afraid of Ibrahim's people nor of Kamrasi, but that as Baker had claimed the country, they must retire. A few days afterwards Kamrasi determined to give the finishing stroke to his enemies. He attacked the neighbouring chief Fowooka, captured the islands on which he resided, massacred the greater number of the inhabitants, and brought away their women and children as slaves. Many of the women were wives of the rebel chiefs, who had never worked laboriously, who were for the most part good-looking, with soft and pleasing expression, brown complexion, fine noses, woolly hair, and good figures. Some old women who had also been captured, and were unable to keep up with their victors on the return march, were killed on the road as being cumbersome. This victory delighted Kamrasi exceedingly, and he sent large quantities of ivory to Ibrahim : a large hut was filled with elephants' tusks of the largest size.

The time arrived for leaving Kisoona. The place was no longer habitable, as the M'was of Uganda had entered the

country, and Kamrasi had fled the village. Mrs. Baker was
carried in a litter, and her husband in a chair. They halted
at the village of Deang. Here the porters deserted. The
next portion of the march to Foweera was both difficult and
dangerous. When they reached the latter village, they found
it in great excitement, as the M'was were reported as only
three miles distant. Here a favourite servant, Richarn, who
was reported killed, returned quite safe. His loss would
have been a heavy one, as he carried the gun of that great
traveller and hunter Oswell. On the 20th September,
Ibrahim arrived with the post from England, which had
come through the Consul at Khartoum. With the exception
of a letter and a copy of the *Illustrated London News* from
Captain Speke, this post was of a two years' old date. The
letters had been brought from Gondokoro by Ibrahim. He
had also thought of other necessities, and had brought a
coarse piece of cotton cloth to make into clothes for Baker,
with a piece of cotton print as a dress for his wife. He
also brought a large jar of honey, some rice and coffee, which
had been left for want of porters at Shooa. Ibrahim now
came into possession of the large stores of ivory which had
been concealed at Kisoona ; Kamrasi also sent an additional
supply to the place where they had halted, within half a mile
of the Victoria Nile. Ibrahim's men assisted Kamrasi in
invading the Langgo country, where Fowooka, his old enemy,
had retreated, and received handsome donations of ivory
in return. These instalments of ivory were, however, more
than paid for by the cattle which he received from the
Turks. These cattle had been plundered from their enemies.
Ibrahim had brought many presents with him from Gondokoro for Kamrasi ; amongst them fifty pounds of beads, a

revolver pistol, cotton cloths, blue glass tumblers, looking-glasses, etc. When the war was finished, Kamrasi determined to destroy all those inhabitants of Foweera who had been in league with his enemies the M'was, and had a number of them executed daily. Baker moralizes thus on the power of this king. In addition to those slaves captured in the various wars, Kamrasi had presented him with seventy-two. 'There never was a more supreme despot,' writes Baker, 'than the king Kamrasi. Not only the property, but the families of his subjects were at his disposal; he boasted that "all belonged to him." Thus, when disposed to be liberal, he took from others and bestowed upon his favourites; should any sufferer complain, there were no lawyer's costs, but the "shoe" or death. His power depended upon a perfect system of espionage, by which he obtained a knowledge of all that passed throughout his kingdom; that being divided into numerous small districts, each governed by a chief, who was responsible for the acts committed within his jurisdiction, the government was wonderfully simplified. Should a complaint be made against a governor, he was summoned before the king; if guilty, death or the "shoe." To be suspected of rebellion was to die. A bodyguard of about five hundred men, who were allowed to pillage the country at discretion, secured the power of the king, as with this organized force always at hand, he could pounce upon the suspected and extinguish them at once; thus the tyrant held his sway over a population so timid that they yielded tamely to his oppression. Having now allied himself to the Turks, he had conceived the most ambitious views of conquering Uganda, and of restoring the ancient kingdom of Kitwara; but the total absence of physical courage will utterly frustrate such plans for extension, and Kamrasi the Cruel will never be known as Kamrasi the Conqueror.'

About the middle of November they bade adieu to Kamrasi, as the Turks with whom they intended to travel were ready to return to Shooa. The amount of ivory was so great that seven hundred porters were required to carry it and the provisions for a five days' march through uninhabited country. Baker had now spent ten months of wretchedness in the country of Unyoro, and was glad to turn his back upon it. The whole party, including women and children, numbered about one thousand. At the end of the fifth day's march, Shooa was reached. They found the change delightful after Unyoro, the vegetation there being wet and dense, while it was now dry, and the grass short and of a fine quality. The native women crowded round the camp to welcome Mrs. Baker, dancing in honour of their return; expecting, however, the present of a cow for their trouble. The time spent at Shooa, Baker employed in rambling about the neighbourhood, climbing the mountain, collecting information, and making duplicates of maps. The Turks had discovered a new country called Lira, about thirty miles from Shooa, where the natives were reported to be extremely friendly. In some of those who were located in the Turks' camp, the head-dress formed a remarkable feature in their general appearance. The hair was woven into a thick felt, which covered the shoulders, and extended as low upon the back as the shoulder-blade. Much of this hair was borrowed, and they were not particular as to the source from whence it was received. Sometimes this head-dress was further plastered and dressed with bluish clay and pipe-clay. The people of Lira were at this time fighting with their neighbours the Langgos—those of Shooa with the natives of Fatiko. The

Khartoum traders had, of course, taken advantage of this
general discord to advance their own interests. The two
leaders of the rival traders' parties—Ibrahim and Mahommed
Wat-el-Mek—had joined themselves with the contending tribes,
and so for miles around Shooa there was but a blackened
wilderness; thousands of cattle had been driven off, and the
natives had fled either to the hills or to other countries. The
natives had been so spoilt, too, by the payment in cows instead
of in beads, that they could not be prevailed upon to act as
porters to Gondokoro under a payment of four cows each. Thus,
according to what was required by the Turks, one thousand
men were needed, for whom a payment of four thousand cows
would be necessary. This led to extreme and violent measures
on the part of the Turks, especially on the part of Debono's
people, who were situated about twenty-five miles distant.
The tribes combined to thwart them, and refused to carry
their ivory to Gondokoro. The chief of Faloro, by name
Werdella, declared open war against them, drove off their
cattle, and retreating to the mountains, challenged them to
rescue them.

'During the absence of the traders' party upon various
expeditions,' Baker further says, 'about fifty men were left
in their camp as headquarters. Nothing could exceed the
brutality of the people. They had erected stills, and produced
a powerful corn spirit from the native mirissa; their entire
time was passed in gambling, drinking, and fighting, both by
night and day. The natives were ill-treated, their female
slaves and children brutally ill-used, and the entire camp was a
mere slice from the infernal regions. My portion of the camp
being a secluded courtyard, we were fortunately independent.'
Baker used his influence against the atrocities which were

being continually committed, and explained to the Turks that he would use force to prevent such acts, and that he would report the names of all those to the Egyptian authorities who should commit any murder that he could prove. At this time he had gained an extraordinary influence over the people, enabling him to exert such authority as saved the lives of many unfortunate creatures who would have perished but for his intervention. Baker's shooting at Shooa was mostly confined to the antelope; whenever an animal was shot, the natives always cut its throat and drank the hot blood as it gushed from the artery. In the rambles in search of game, he recognised two kinds of cotton indigenous to the country—one with a yellow blossom, which proved comparatively worthless; the other with a red blossom, producing a fine quality, easily detachable from the seeds.

In the month of February 1865, Baker and his party, with the traders' company, left Shooa for Gondokoro. The camp was full of ivory; the total results of the ivory campaign for the last two months had yielded upwards of 32,000 lbs., equal to about £9630 when delivered in Egypt. The largest portion of Ibrahim's immense store of ivory had been given to him by Kamrasi. Baker had guaranteed him 10,000 lbs. of ivory should he quit Obbo and go southwards with him, and he had received more than three times that amount. It was a trial to part with several of the slave children, to whom they had grown attached. The road for several days was through beautiful park-like lands, arriving at the point of junction between the Un-y-Amé and the Nile. About three miles from this point of junction between these rivers stood a tamarind tree, which was, up till the date of Baker's expedition, the farthest southern limit previously reached by any traveller from the north. Here Signor Miani's expedition had been obliged to halt, being deceived by his escort, which had refused to proceed farther. Travelling onwards, from a rocky height about 800 feet high, they could discern the course of the Nile from w.s.w. for about twenty miles winding through marshy ground. The country opposite to where they stood was Koshi, which formed the west bank of the Nile, extending the whole way to the Albert lake. The country they occupied at the time was Madi, which extended as the east bank of the Nile to the angle of the Victoria Nile junction, opposite Magungo. Opposite the summit of the pass from which they scanned the country, rose Gebel Kookoo, 2500 feet high, a prominent feature in the chain of mountains bordering the west bank, until within thirty miles of Gondokoro. The mouth of the Un-y-Amé is the navigable limit of the river from the Albert lake.

Baker was now on the track by which Speke and Grant returned. The Nile, entering the valley between Gebel Kookoo and the western range, is obstructed in its course by numerous rocky islets, and mud banks covered with papyrus rush, causing the stream to widen out to about a mile. Below this spot a short distance the channel rapidly contracted, becoming a roaring torrent in its passage through a narrow gorge. Still following the Nile banks, several waterfalls were seen, 'through which for many miles the angry Nile chafed and roared like a lion in its confined den.' On crossing the Asua river, they became aware that they had entered the territory of the hostile Bari tribe. The route led over a fine country on a line with the Nile, with a rock-bound channel to the west of the march. In passing through a gorge between low rocky hills, they were attacked by a party

of the Bari tribe, who discharged poisoned arrows at them.
The natives were easily kept at bay, however, and they
encamped in safety in an open clearing beyond. The next
day they were followed again by the natives, who only waited
an opportunity to attack them.   In the evening they occupied two small deserted villages.   Here a night attack was
made by the natives, and poisoned arrows were thrown into
the camp, but the affair ended when one of the men was
shot by a sentry.   Marching fifteen miles a day from this
point, the mountains around Gondokoro, familiar to him
when starting two years previously, now dawned upon him.
Resting within three miles of Gondokoro, that night was full
of speculations as to whether there would be a boat waiting
for him with letters and supplies.   Money had been left
with an agent at Khartoum for this purpose.   Next morning,
starting ahead of Ibrahim and his party, the English flag
leading the way, his men cheering and firing salutes, they
were met by a party of the Turks from Gondokoro.   Much
to his disappointment, neither boats, supplies, nor letters
awaited Baker.   He had long since been given up as dead
by the inhabitants of Khartoum.   Others suggested that he
might have gone to Zanzibar, but the prevalent opinion was
that he was killed.   'At this cold and barren reply,' writes
Baker, 'I felt almost choked.   We had looked forward to
arriving at Gondokoro as to a home; we had expected that
a boat would have been sent on the chance of finding us, as
I had left money in the hands of an agent in Khartoum;
but there was literally nothing to receive us, and we were
helpless to return.   We had worked for years in misery, such
as I have but faintly described, to overcome the difficulties
of this hitherto unconquerable exploration; we had suc-

ceeded, and what was the result? Not even a letter from
home to welcome us if alive! As I sat beneath a tree, and
looked down upon the glorious Nile that flowed a few yards
beneath my feet, I pondered upon the value of my toil.
I had traced the river to its great Albert source, and as the
mighty stream glided before me, the mystery that had ever
shrouded its origin was dissolved. I no longer looked upon
its waters with a feeling approaching to awe, for I knew its
home, and had visited its cradle. Had I overrated the
importance of the discovery? and had I wasted some of
the best years of my life to obtain a shadow? I recalled to recollection the practical question of Commoro,
the chief of Latooka, "Suppose you get to the great
lake, what will you do with it? What will be the good of
it? If you find that the large river does flow from it, what
then?"'

The news which had already come from Khartoum was
neither bright nor reassuring. The different trading parties
now arrived in Gondokoro had with them upwards of three
thousand slaves. The message regarding these was to the
effect that the Egyptian authorities had received orders from
the European powers to stop the slave trade. Four vessels
had arrived at Khartoum from Cairo; two of them had
ascended the White Nile, and had captured many slavers.
Their crews had been imprisoned, and subjected to the
bastinado and torture. An Egyptian regiment had been
stationed in the Shillook country; steamers were cruising to
intercept any boats from the interior in their descent to
Khartoum. The plague was also raging at Khartoum; 15,000
people had fallen victims to its ravages. The White Nile, by
a freak of nature, was dammed up; and the crews of several

vessels were occupied in endeavouring to cut a passage through the obstruction.

The discomfiture of the traders at this news was very great, and they were prepared for flight into the interior. Baker secured a boat from one of the traders for £40, and arranged to leave at once, after cleansing his vessel as thoroughly as possible, several persons having died of the plague within it in the journey from Khartoum. Baker had secured great influence over these traders, as the greater part of what he had promised had been performed, and most of his predictions had been realized. He also received the credit of the present interference in the slave traffic by having written to the Consul-General of Egypt in 1863. They were completely cowed, however, and made no attempt at retaliation. Indeed, much of their good luck in ivory-hunting was credited to him; disaster had befallen all who had been against him. Crowds lined the cliff and the high ground as they bade good-bye to the station, with the English flag flying at the mast-head. Grateful to Divine Providence that had so shielded and protected them, they glided down the current of the Nile, past the endless marshes, with hearts less full of triumph than of calm content. There was now ample leisure to write letters to England, to be posted at Khartoum; and one of the pleasures awaiting him was the meeting with Captain Speke, when he could explain how completely he had accomplished the task which he had undertaken. Baker has thus summarized his discoveries up till that time.

'The Nile,' he writes, 'cleared of its mystery, resolves itself into comparative simplicity. The actual basin of the Nile is included between about 22° and 39° east longitude, and from 3° south to 18° north latitude. The drainage of that vast area is monopolized by the Egyptian river. The Victoria and Albert lakes, the two great equatorial reservoirs, are the recipients of all affluents south of the equator, the Albert lake being the grand reservoir in which are concentrated the entire waters from the south, in addition to tributaries from the Blue Mountains from the north of the equator. The Albert Nyanza is the great basin of the Nile. The distinction between that and the Victoria Nyanza is that the Victoria is a reservoir receiving the eastern affluents, and it becomes a starting-point, or the most elevated *source* at the point where the river issues from it at the Ripon Falls; the Albert is a reservoir not only receiving the western and southern affluents direct from the Blue Mountains, but it also receives the supply from the Victoria and from the entire equatorial Nile basin. The Nile, as it issues from the Albert Nyanza, is the *entire* Nile; prior to its birth from the Albert lake, it is *not* the entire Nile. A glance at the map will at once exemplify the relative value of the two great lakes. The Victoria gathers all the waters on the eastern side and sheds them into the northern extremity of the Albert; while the latter, from its character and position, is the direct channel of the Nile that receives all waters that belong to the equatorial Nile basin. Thus the Victoria is the first source; but from the Albert the river issues at once as the great White Nile.' Thus Baker finished the discoveries made by Speke and Grant. These travellers had traced the country from Zanzibar to the northern water-shed of Africa. They settled that the Ripon Falls, flowing from the Victoria Nyanza, were the highest source of the Nile. They traced the course of the river to Karuma Falls, and again met the Nile in lat. 3° 32′ N. They were told that it flowed into the Luta N'Zige, or Albert Nyanza; but it remained for Baker to describe and verify this supposition, as he has so ably done. The rainfall, to within 3° north of the equator, extends over ten months, beginning in February and terminating in the end of November. The heaviest rains fall from April to the end of August; during the last two months of this season the rivers are at their largest. The rivers are thus kept constant throughout the year; the Albert lake continues at a high level, yielding a steady volume to the Nile. The geological formation of Central Africa shows an altitude of 4000 feet above the sea level, with no indication amongst its prevailing granitic and sandstone rocks that it has ever been submerged, or subjected to any sea change.

Khartoum was reached on the 5th May 1865, when he received a welcome from the entire European population on the following morning. Sad to relate, his faithful boy Saat had died of the plague on the river. Another sad event was the death of Captain Speke, the tidings of which he had just now heard. The Blue Nile was now so low that they could not descend. The camels used in land transport were also dead. Two months of waiting had therefore to be undergone in Khartoum, subject to the intense heat and constant dust-storms.

The measures taken by the European powers for the suppression of the slave traffic led to the capture of two vessels laden with 850 human beings, packed together, as Baker relates, like anchovies, the living and the dying festering together, and the dead lying beneath them. 'European eye-witnesses,' he writes, 'assured me that the disembarking of this frightful cargo could not be adequately described. The slaves were in a state of starvation, having had nothing to eat for several days. They were landed in Khartoum; the dead, and many of the dying, were tied by the ankles, and dragged along the ground by donkeys through the streets. The most malignant typhus, or plague, had been engendered among this mass of filth and misery, thus closely packed together. Upon landing, the women were divided by the Egyptian authorities among the soldiers. These creatures brought the plague to Khartoum, which, like a curse visited upon this country of slavery and abomination, spread like a fire throughout the town, and consumed the regiments that had received this horrible legacy from the dying cargo of slaves.' While staying in the town, Baker discovered Mahommed Her, the headman of Chenooda's party, who had incited his men to mutiny, and had taken the deserters into his employ. He had him arrested and brought before the Divan, when Mahommed was sentenced to be flogged.

On 1st July they left Khartoum for Berber. They had a narrow escape from shipwreck in the cataracts of the Nile ; but Berber was reached in safety, when Baker received a warm welcome from a French gentleman and his wife, who had been resident for many years in the Soudan. From thence they took the route overland to Souakim, a considerable town on the Red Sea, where the houses are all built of coral. From this place they made the voyage in five days to Suez. Letters awaited him at the British Consulate, one of which informed him that the Royal Geographical Society had awarded him the Victoria Gold Medal for his exertions. This was all the more gratifying, as it was bestowed before they had become aware of the success of the expedition.

Having introduced his faithful black servant Richarn to a comfortable situation in a hotel in Suez, the journey ended. 'The past,' he writes, 'appeared like a dream :

the rushing sound of the train renewed ideas of civilisation.
Had I really come from the Nile sources? It was no
dream. A witness sat before me: a face still young, but
bronzed like an Arab with years of exposure to a burning
sun; haggard and worn with toil and sickness, and shaded
with cares happily now past; the devoted companion of my
pilgrimage, to whom I owed success and life—my wife.'

SIR SAMUEL WHITE BAKER, M.A., F.R.G.S.

PART II.

Expedition to Central Africa for the Suppression of the Slave Trade under Ismail, Khedive of Egypt.

IT has not unfrequently happened in the case of the individual, some special training gone through, or some special experience, has been a preparation for higher and more useful work. A door of usefulness opens to him who is prepared and ready to enter it. The explorations of Sir Samuel White Baker at the Nile sources had given him a useful experience, which was to be utilized in an important expedition for the suppression of the slave trade; and although this expedition may not have been so fruitful in results as was expected, yet he has laid bare a great tract of country hitherto imperfectly known. Baker, from what he knew and had personally seen of the odious slave traffic, concluded that until this blighting scourge was removed, true prosperity and commercial enterprise was impossible in Central Africa.

So emphatic are the horrors of the traffic, that to the country subjected to them he uses the one strong word 'ruin.' Those engaged in the traffic were for the most part Arabs, and subjects of the Egyptian Government. Deserting

their agricultural employments in the Soudan, they united themselves into companies in the pay of different merchants of
Khartoum.   It was computed, before the expedition was
determined upon, that about 15,000 of the subjects of the
Khedive of Egypt were engaged in the ivory trade and slave-
hunting on the White Nile.   At a moderate calculation, fifty
thousand slaves were drawn from Central Africa by way of
the White Nile annually.   While travelling in Egypt in
company with their Royal Highnesses the Prince and
Princess of Wales, the Khedive at that time determined
to strike a blow at the slave trade of the White Nile.   Sir
Samuel Baker was appealed to in order to sketch out a plan
for the proposed expedition to Central Africa, and in due
time he was placed in full command of it by the issue of
a firman from Ismail the Khedive.   Its chief provisions were
as follows :—

' To subdue to our authority the countries situated to the
south of Gondokoro ;

' To suppress the slave trade; to introduce a system of
regular commerce ;

' To open to navigation the great lakes of the equator ;

' And to establish a chain of military stations and commercial depots, distant at intervals of three days' march,
throughout Central Africa, accepting Gondokoro as the base
of operations.

' The supreme command of this expedition is confided to
Sir Samuel White Baker for four years, commencing from
1st April 1869 ; on whom also we confer the most absolute
and supreme power, even that of death, over all those who
may compose the expedition.

We confer upon him the same absolute and supreme

authority over all those countries belonging to the Nile basin south of Gondokoro.'

·The purpose of the expedition was, as may be supposed, looked upon with suspicion and dislike by the interested classes in Egypt. The sons of the Khedive and his two ministers, Nubar Pasha and Cherif Pasha (an Armenian and a Circassian), gave him their firm support. Having received full powers, Baker gave orders that the following vessels be fitted up with engines of the best construction, which were to be carried across the Nubian desert in plates and sections :—

No. 1. A paddle steamer of 251 tons, 32 horse-power.

No. 2. A twin-screw high-pressure steamer of 20 horse-power, 108 tons.

No. 3. A twin-screw high-pressure steamer of 10 horse-power, 38 tons.

Nos. 4 and 5. Two steel lifeboats, each 30 feet by 9 = 10 tons each.

For the success of such an expedition, the utmost care and thoughtfulness was required in the preparation for the enterprise. Here his former African experience proved invaluable. Besides himself and Lady Baker, the English party were : Lieutenant Julian Alleyne Baker, R.N. ; Mr. Edwin Higginbotham, civil engineer; Mr. Wood, secretary ; Dr. Joseph Gedge, physician ; Mr. Marcopolo, chief storekeeper and interpreter ; Mr. M'William, chief engineer of steamers ; Mr. Jarvis, chief shipwright ; with other shipwrights, boilermaker, and two servants. About £9000 was spent in providing stores for four years. Four galvanized iron magazines, each eighty feet long by twenty in width, were provided in order to protect the materials necessary for the expedition ; these were of the most miscellaneous, but at the same time perfect description. The magazines, he declared, could produce anything, from a needle to a crowbar, or from a handkerchief to a boat's sail. The supplies from England had indeed been so carefully arranged that scarcely a want was felt on the journey but could be supplied. Various delays were experienced before the expedition was arranged to start in three divisions. Thirty-six vessels, including six steamers, were to ascend the cataracts of the Nile to Khartoum, conveying the merchandise. Twenty-five vessels were to be ready, together with three steamers, by the time this fleet should arrive. There was also to be a desert transport from Korosko to Khartoum, under the charge of the chief engineer. Baker himself was to bring up the rear, by way of Souakim on the Red Sea, to Berber. The military force under command comprised 1645 troops, including a corps of 200 irregular cavalry, and two batteries of artillery. The ammunition and other perishable goods were well packed. Medicines and drugs were on hand of the best quality.

Sir Samuel White Baker, bringing up the rear of the expedition, left Suez on 5th December 1869, reaching Khartoum in the short space of thirty-two days, including stoppages. While there was no external change in Khartoum, yet the district between that town and Berber bore unmistakeable marks of neglect. The river's bank, formerly so highly cultivated, was now a wilderness. Oppression had driven the inhabitants from the soil. 'This terrible desolation,' writes Baker, 'was caused by the Governor-General of the Soudan, who, although himself an honest man, trusted too much to the honesty of others, who preyed upon the inhabitants. As a good and true Mohammedan, he left his territory to the sole care of God ; and thus, trusting in Providence, he simply increased the taxes. In one year he sent to the Khedive, his master, £100,000 in hard dollars, wrung from the poor peasantry, who must have lost an equal amount in the pillage that accompanies the collection.' The result had been that those who had thus been overtaxed and plundered had betaken themselves to plunder others, in carrying out the system of brigandage on the White Nile which Baker's expedition was intended to suppress.

The transport vessels which were ordered to be ready at Khartoum were found to be awanting, much to the chagrin of the chief of the expedition ; the Governor-General giving as a reason that it was impossible to procure the number of vessels required, and as he had purchased a house for Baker, he trusted that he would not start until the following season. Baker, however, insisted on the purchase of vessels, and in a few weeks thirty-three vessels were caulked, rigged, and ready for the voyage of 1450 miles to Gondokoro. Only part of the force of troops could, however, be taken at this time ; the remainder were to be sent on Mr. Higginbotham's arrival. The cavalry, on being reviewed, were left behind as useless.

The flotilla, consisting of two steamers and thirty-one sailing vessels, with a military force of about eight hundred men, at length left Khartoum on the 8th February 1870. Dropping down the Blue Nile, they at length steamed up the White Nile, fairly under weigh, after one month had been wasted in preparation. The news had reached him by this time that Mr. Higginbotham had arrived with the steel steamers for the Albert Nyanza. The following entry occurs in his journal of 8th February :—' The usual

Egyptian delays have entirely thwarted my plans. No vessels have arrived from Cairo, as they only started on 29th August. Thus, rather than turn back, I start with a mutilated expedition, without a single transport arrival.' In a hundred and three hours and ten minutes' steaming, Fashooda was reached, being 618 miles by river from Khartoum. This fortified town was garrisoned by a regiment of Egyptian soldiers, under the command of Ali Bey, a Kurd. The governor reported that his country was in excellent order, as he had received instructions from the Khedive to exert himself against the slave trade. A month's rations were taken in here, and starting again, the junction of the Sobat was reached on 16th February. The Sobat supplies a large and powerful volume of water to the White Nile. Passing this junction, the character of the river changes, as the traveller now enters upon a region of immense flats and boundless marshes. They reached the junction of the Bahr Giraffe on 17th February, and waited here for the arrival of the fleet. That river was to be their new passage instead of the White Nile, but it was curiously obstructed by masses of vegetation. The whole river had become a marsh, beneath which the river oozed through innumerable channels. Sport was not entirely forgotten, as up to this time Baker had killed a hippopotamus, two crocodiles, two pelicans, and twenty-two ducks with the rifle. The Bahr Giraffe proved to be very deep, averaging about nineteen feet, winding through a perfectly flat prairie country, diversified with forest. The mosquitoes proved terribly troublesome to every one. Occasionally the river would be choked by drift vegetation, when all hands had to clear a passage through the obstructions.

On 1st March the whole fleet was forced to come to a dead

stop, as the river, although fourteen feet immediately before, had entirely disappeared in a sea of high grass. After some delay, thirty vessels were ordered to form in line, single file, and cut a pathway through the morass. Seven hundred men were at work on 9th March, slashing through the vegetation with swords and knives, and pulling out the rubbish, which they piled up on either side. Fish were caught in the marshy river, and a hippopotamus was shot with an explosive shell from a rifle ; the shell was an invention of Sir Samuel's. By 21st March they had cut away six miles of vegetation, but they had been hard at work for thirteen days with a thousand men, and they had only made twelve miles. The hard work and the smell from the rotting vegetation and the stinking morass laid many of them aside with fever. On 26th March, one hundred and fifty men were on the sick list, and a despairing feeling began to possess the most of them. This hopeless navigation amongst grass and water-weeds was continued until the end of the month. At the beginning of April the task became more hopeless, and it became apparent that the passage could only be made at the end of December, when the river was full. On 2d April, a further attempt at advance was found to be absurd, and accordingly, Baker determined to return to the Shillock country and found a station. A start might probably be made with the entire force about the end of November. The order to return was therefore given at once, the officers and men concluding that this would probably terminate the expedition. To vary the monotony of the voyage, Baker enjoyed some good sport in the downward passage, killing the antelope, hippopotamus, crocodile, some geese, and ducks.

Arriving at the station of Kutchuk Ali on 13th April, Baker

sent for his agent and explained to him the object of his mission, and recommended him not to send cargoes of slaves down to Khartoum, as he had done in previous years. They arrived at the White Nile on 19th April, when they discovered three vessels belonging to the Governor of Fashooda, Ali Bey, the Koordi. Although he had disclaimed all connection with the slave trade to Baker in the upward journey, he was discovered now to have on hand one hundred and fifty-five slaves. Of these, seventy-one were concealed in the boat, and eighty-four were on shore guarded by sentries. It was discovered also that he made a considerable fortune by levying toll upon every slave brought down the river. This amount he pocketed himself. In the blandest manner possible, Ali Bey had endeavoured to throw dust in the eyes of those connected with the expedition; but this was found to be impossible. He admitted that he was collecting the taxes, and that these slaves were only held as hostages until they should pay their taxes. Many of the slave women were secured to each other by ropes passed from neck to neck; and a crowd of children, including very young infants, were squatted amongst the mass. Baker insisted on the liberation of every slave, adding that he would report the conduct of Ali Bey to the Khedive, from whom he had his authority. Eleven vessels in full sail arrived while these negotiations were pending; it turned out to be that section of the expedition under the charge of Mr. Higginbotham. They were all in good health, and, in company with Lieutenant Baker and Mr. Higginbotham, a visit was paid to the camp of Ali Bey. 'I ordered,' he writes, 'the ropes, irons, and other accompaniments of slavery to be detached; and I explained, through an interpreter, to the astonished crowd of captives, that the Khedive had abolished slavery, therefore they were at liberty to return to their own homes. At first they appeared astounded, and evidently could not realize the fact; but upon my asking them where their homes were, they pointed to the boundless rows of villages in the distance, and said, "These are our homes; but many of our men are killed, and all our cattle and corn are carried off." I could only advise them to pack off as quickly as possible, now that they had the chance of freedom. The women immediately took up their little infants (one had been born during the night), others led the very small children by the hand, and, with a general concert, they burst into the long, quavering, and shrill yell that denotes rejoicing. I watched them as they retreated over the plain to their deserted homes, and I took a coldly-polite farewell of the Koordi.'

Continuing the voyage, a suitable spot of ground was chosen on the banks of the White Nile on which to prepare a station, where they might remain until the Nile was navigable. The place was named Tewfikeeyah, after the Khedive's eldest son, Mahomed Tewfik Pasha. The place rapidly assumed a civilised aspect; the engineers and carpenters were soon busy at work. The ground was well drained. A quay about 500 yards in length was constructed on the banks of the river, where the whole fleet could lie, or embark and disembark their cargoes. Stables were made for the horses and donkeys. The three magazines of galvanized iron, about 80 feet in length, were completed, and the stores from the vessels were lodged within them. Rats came in thousands, attracted by the corn, rice, and other eatables; these, with the white ants, proved unspeakably troublesome. Gardens were prepared, fenced off, and European seeds of various kinds were sown. Baker did not build a house for himself, preferring the com-

fortable diahbeeah moored alongside the garden. A walk led
to two large shady mimosas, where all visitors were received.
A steam sawmill was set up, and boat-building was commenced. In the flat and uninteresting country with which
they were surrounded, timber was scarce,—forest and bush
formed but a fringe on the banks of the river, and the only
large trees were a species of mimosa.

On 1st May, when the camp was being formed, they
received a visit from the King of the Shillooks, Quat Kare.
He was accompanied by two of his wives, four daughters, and
a retinue of about seventy people. He was tall and thin in
appearance; and as his wardrobe was old and scanty, Baker
had him clad in a long blue skirt, an Indian scarf to wear
as a waistband, and a fez. He sat down on a carpet, upon
which he invited his family to sit near him. He did not at
first appear to possess powers of speech, simply fixing his eyes
on Baker and his wife, and then upon the officers in attend-
ance. A question being asked of him, it was replied to by
his wife, a woman apparently about sixty years of age. The
account which she gave of the intrigues of the Governor of
Fashooda gives, according to Baker, an average picture of
Soudan rule.

On the east side of the river, where they had formed their
settlement, it was almost entirely uninhabited. The present
Governor of Fashooda was in a great degree responsible for
this condition of things, as in the slave raids he had made
on the Dinka country, the tribe had been well-nigh exterminated. In riding over the country, it was no uncommon
thing for Baker to discover fragments of broken pottery,
vestiges of former villages. A male ostrich was shot in this
neighbourhood, the first and last which our traveller ever

bagged. The plumage, as usual in the male, was black, with white feathers in the wings and tail. In the stomach of the bird were found scorpions, beetles, leaves of trees, and white, rounded quartz pebbles. The camp began to be crowded with natives, who proved themselves sharp at bargain-making. They exchanged raw cotton and provisions for all kinds of cotton manufactures and iron. Baker bestowed on the natives . some good Egyptian cotton-seed, also the seed of various European vegetables. The soldiers at the station were in the habit of giving their corn to the Shillooks to grind, and they invariably returned with the proper complement of flour. An old blind Sheik met his death in returning from marketing. His canoe was bitten and upset by a hippopotamus in the river, and he himself was so lacerated that death ensued.

On the 10th May a sail appeared up the river, which appeared to be approaching on her way to Khartoum. Baker sent his trusty aide-de-camp, Colonel Abd-el-Kader, on board to make the necessary inquiries. The vessel, according to the captain and the vakeel (agent and commander of station), was laden with corn, with ivory beneath the corn for the supply of the crew and the soldiers. Colonel Abd-el-Kader was, however, not easily deceived. Probing amongst the corn with a steel ramrod from a soldier's rifle, a smothered cry was elicited, and a negro woman was afterwards dragged forth. The forecastle and stern had been boarded up; and when the planking was removed, a mass of humanity,—boys, girls, and women,—closely packed like herrings in a barrel, was revealed to view. They had been kept silent under fear of threats. A young woman was also found sewn up in the sail attached to the mainyard of the vessel to avoid discovery. When the vessel was unloaded, one hundred and fifty slaves were discovered to have been concealed on board; as they had been stowed into an inconceivably small space, the stench was found to be horrible.

Baker gave orders that the vakeel and the captain of the vessel should be put in irons. Much to the astonishment of the slaves, those in irons were liberated. The ivory having been weighed and the tusks counted, the vessel was reloaded, with an officer and guard on board, who had orders to confiscate her as a slaver on reaching Khartoum. The slaves were ordered to wash, and clothes were issued for the naked women. A paper of freedom, signed by Baker, was given to each. This was put in a hollow reed and suspended round the neck. Those negresses who wished to marry with any of the young men in the regiments were at liberty to do so. The women who remained single were employed in domestic work, and in cooking for the troops. The boys were divided into classes, and apprenticed to various kinds of work. Mostoora, a precocious little girl of about three years of age, but quicker than most girls of double her age, was adopted by Mrs. Baker.

The Egyptian troops, while at the station, continued to be sickly and dispirited, going about their work in a slouching way. To the soldiers and sailors, in order to keep them from inaction, was given the employment of cultivating a portion of the land around the station.

Baker started again on 11th August 1870, to explore the obstructions in the main Nile, in the hope of discovering some passage through them. A small channel was discovered, taking them to the Bahr Gazal. The latter proved to be but an extraordinary series of lakes and swamps, changing their appearance every year. Baker, with remarkable foresight, contradicted the opinion entertained by Dr. Livingstone, that the river Lualaba, which he had discovered south-west of Lake Tanganyika, was an affluent of the Bahr Gazal, and quite correctly concluded that it might possibly be an affluent of the Congo. The discoveries of H. M. Stanley, in crossing Africa, have proved the latter to be indeed the Congo river. Having been absent about ten days, he returned, resolved that the main channel of the Nile must be cleared from the huge rafts of vegetation before navigation could be possible. Any attempt to civilise Central Africa, and annex new territory, would be useless until a proper channel should be opened for regular communication. He now determined that the expedition should start for the south on 1st December, and proceeded to Khartoum to make the necessary arrangements. The measures already taken against the slave trade had rendered the expedition unpopular; but worse than this, it was now discovered that the entire White Nile was rented by the traders. This placed our traveller in the position of attempting to annex a country already leased out by the Government to those who carried on the slave trade. The leases bound the tenant to abstain from slave-hunting; but when away from legitimate authority, they acted pretty much as they pleased. 'If the owner of a pack of wolves,' writes Baker, 'were to send them on a commission to gather wool from a flock of sheep, with the simple protection of such parting advice as, "Begone, good wolves, behave yourselves like lambs, and do not hurt the mutton!" the proprietor of the pack would be held responsible for the acts of his wolves. This was the situation in the Soudan. The entire country was leased out to piratical slave-hunters, under the name of traders, by the Khartoum Government; and although the rent, in the shape of large sums of money, had been received for years into the treasury of the Soudan, my expedition was to explode like a shell among the traders, and would at once annihilate the trade.' The Khedive was thoroughly sincere in his endeavours to put down the slave trade as far as he was individually concerned, only he was placed in a false position by the traders and Governor of the Soudan. Finding that Ali Bey of Fashooda had been concerned in the slave trade, as proved by Baker, he was dismissed from his service.

On 10th October 1870 the start was again made for the south, arriving at their former station, Tewfikeeyah, on 22d October. It was now definitely arranged that the first part of the fleet would be started for Gondokoro on 1st December. Towards the end of October, several vessels, in attempting to pass the station with slaves, were captured and detained, and the slaves liberated. They did not behave very handsomely to their liberators, however, as they not only ran away during the night with the new clothes given them by the Government, but they also stole some of the soldiers' kits. The brutal treatment they have undergone has helped to do away with all moral distinctions in their own minds: the fact of their having been so frequently deceived has made them incapable of understanding the truth.

The station of Tewfikeeyah was finally left behind on 11th December. The fleet consisted of fifty-nine vessels, in which were stowed away all the goods from the station. Nothing was left save a few rows of deserted huts. The sad news of the death of Dr. Gedge at Khartoum was a decided loss to the expedition. The Shillook country was now at peace; the Governor of Fashooda had been disgraced, and Quat Kare had again been appointed chief of the country in room of the pretender Jangy. The river was very full at starting, which augured well for the voyage. The Egyptian troops, however, appeared dispirited. Two vessels were sunk shortly after starting, which gave Baker occasion to observe: 'To work in this country is simply heart-breaking; the material is utterly worthless—boats, officers, and men are all alike. The loss of invaluable time is ruinous, and the ignorance of the people is such that they can do nothing by themselves; thus I must be everywhere and superintend everything personally.' One of the largest and finest vessels of the fleet, which had been sunk near the junction of the Sobat and Nile, was laden with steamer sections and machinery, the losing of which would have been fatal to the success of the expedition. With great difficulty and loss of time the cargo and the vessel were saved. Another great aggravation was the listless way in which the natives in charge of the fleet had performed their duties. Both officers and men idled their time on the passage. On 8th January they were stopped by floating rafts of vegetation, through which a passage had to be cut; and on till nearly the end of March the passage through the masses of vegetation was extremely difficult. At last they gained the channel of the White Nile, when Gondokoro was reached on 15th April 1871.

They found the country round Gondokoro sadly changed since their last visit. Villages had been destroyed, and the natives driven for refuge to numerous low islands of the river through the attacks of the people of Loquia at the instigation of the traders. The chief, Alloran, was sent for, and he promised to urge his people to return for protection, cultivate the corn, and build the huts promised for the troops upon arrival. He afterwards took a sullen fit, however, and showed

most unmistakeably that his mind had been prejudiced against
them by the slave traders. The Austrian Mission Station was
completely dismantled, and thousands of lemons had fallen
from the trees only to grow withered and neglected. The
natives had ground down the bricks as a powder wherewith to
smear their bodies. The building of a station was commenced, and the cultivation of a large garden was also begun.
In this garden were sown onions, radishes, beans, spinach,
water melons, sweet melons, cucumbers, oranges, custard
apples, Indian corn, garlic, barmian, tobacco, cabbages, tomatoes, chillies, carrots, parsley, celery. The soldiers and sailors
worked at gardening from 6 A.M. till 11 ; the remainder of
the day they were at liberty to devote to the construction of
their own huts. Gardening, Baker felt to have a localizing and
civilising effect upon those who were engaged in it, and he
was thus fain to encourage it by every means in his power.
His impression was that the young missionary would succeed
much better when he carried on some such agricultural work
side by side with the savage.

There was a forest of magnificent tamarind trees in the
neighbourhood of the station. One of these trees, about a
mile from the station, could have sheltered within its shadow
about a thousand cattle. The intractable nature of the Bari
natives, upon whose land they had settled, may be gathered
from the conversation which took place with the chief. Sheik
Alloran would neither sell, nor allow any of his men to sell,
sheep or cattle to any of the troops. He sent some of his
men to work before them when engaged in gardening operations, in order that they might claim a right to the soil. The
following conversation, as related by Baker, then took place :—

'How long are you going to remain here?' he asked. He

continued, 'You had better go back to Khartoum, and I will eat the corn you have planted when it becomes ripe.'

Baker explained that Gondokoro would henceforth be head-quarters for troops, and that they should cultivate a large extent for corn. In reply to the question as to whom the land belonged, it was explained that they had been driven from it by superior force, and that now it was under the protection of the Khedive.

He replied, 'Who does this tree belong to?' (they were standing beneath its shade).

'It belongs to the Khedive of Egypt,' replied Baker, 'who is now protector of the whole country, and I am his repre-sentative to establish his government.'

He replied: 'Then you had better be off to Khartoum, for we don't want any government here.'

Baker found the Bari country thickly inhabited, although there was no cohesion amongst the natives; each district had its distinct chief. The general feature of the land was rolling park-like grass lands, with forests containing excellent timber. Their dwelling-places were usually very neat, each hut being surrounded by a small court made of cement composed of clay from the white ant-hills mixed with cow-dung and ashes. The Baris are a pastoral people, possessing great herds of cattle. These cattle, as well as the sheep, are small and active. All their operations are conducted by signals given by the drum, which with them answers the purpose of the bugle-call in ordinary military movements. The drum is exactly the shape of an egg with a slice taken off the upper end. A certain number of beats answers the purpose of a signal for the milking of the cows, while a beat in another style is given when the country is in danger of invasion. Their weapons are finely-wrought

III.   G

lances, and bows with barbed arrows. The men are tall and powerful, always naked and smeared with ashes. The women wear aprons before and behind. Salt is one of the commodities which they were in the habit of selling to natives of the interior.

It soon became evident at the station that the Baris were hostile to them. Their whole demeanour from the beginning had been unfriendly. Although there were thousands of cattle feeding before their very eyes, not one of them was purchasable. Their policy, pursued at the instigation of the traders, was to starve the troops, so that they would be obliged to evacuate the position and return to Khartoum.

On 26th May 1871, the ceremony of the official annexation of Gondokoro was gone through by Baker and his men, in the presence of the natives. A flagstaff about eighty feet high had been erected on the highest point of land overlooking the river. The plain had been cleared of brushwood, and 1200 men marched from the station at Gondokoro in clean uniforms, to take part in the ceremony. The official proclamation describing the annexation of the country to Egypt, in the name of the Khedive, was read at the foot of the flagstaff. The Ottoman flag was then run up the halyards, the officers with drawn swords saluted the flag, the troops presented arms, the batteries of artillery fired a royal salute, and then the ceremony was complete. The troops afterwards marched past in order for a supposed attack on an enemy, and fired away about ten thousand rounds of blank cartridge. After being dispersed, the remainder of the day was spent as a holiday by the men. Baker had a large dinner party that day, to which fourteen of the officers were invited. Roast beef and plum-pudding, and other good things, were indulged in. Dinner over, Lieutenant Baker amused both officers and men by a magic-lantern entertainment. One of the scenes most applauded was Moses going through the Red Sea with the Israelites, which had to be twice displayed.

The sheik of the Baris around Gondokoro, having been warned, if he still allowed his cattle to graze on the forbidden side of the river, that they would be confiscated, entirely disobeyed orders, and two hundred head of cattle were captured. On promising to bring thatch grass, and assist the troops to form the station, their cattle were returned. Their promise of assistance was never kept, however, as they positively refused to work. They would have been gratified if Baker would have consented to attack the enemy of their tribe, Lorquia, by which means cattle and sheep would have been obtained both for themselves and for the station. All attempts to preach morality to them were hopeless; they simply advised him to 'take women and cattle, and then the natives would listen to my advice, but not otherwise.' On 1st June, it became evident that hostilities might be expected. A general order was issued to the troops, to the effect that the natives of the Bari had disobeyed the summons of the Government, had refused compliance with the regulations established, and that it had become necessary to compel them to obedience by force. In the event of an outbreak, the soldiers were forbidden on pain of death to capture women or children of either sex.

The natives had begun to annoy the sentries, and endeavoured to drive off their cattle by stealth. They appeared to have deserted their villages on the island opposite to the camp, so Baker determined to pay it a visit in return for the attacks which were continually being made. This affair ended in the capture of some cattle. Not only were the Baris exceedingly troublesome, but they leagued themselves with the natives of Belinian against them. One day the natives of the latter place made a sudden rush upon the cattle guards, shooting one soldier with an arrow, and wounding another with a lance. An order was given at once for an attack on Belinian. Baker left the station on horseback, accompanied by Lieutenant Baker, Mr. Higginbotham, with Lieutenant-Colonel Abd-el-Kader, and twenty men from the detachment called the 'Forty Thieves.' Four companies, with one gun, were added to these from headquarters. A night march was undertaken, when they arrived in the neighbourhood of Belinian in early morning. A stockade, or zareeba, was stormed, and a prize of six hundred cows secured. A fat calf was killed, as the men were hungry, and the cooking began. The fat, kidneys, and liver, having been cut into pieces about two inches square and arranged on a steel ramrod, were well salted and peppered, and laid on the red-hot embers. The ramrod is then stuck upright in the ground, and the meat eaten off as required. The cows gave milk in plenty; so, in the meantime, the camp was well supplied. Three young girls who had been captured were released. The Baris kept aloof, merely watching their movements from the tops of high trees. The cattle were driven over safely to Gondokoro without further trouble from the natives.

On 9th June, Abou Saood, a noted slave trader, arrived with eight vessels opposite the island in the river. In his passage up the river, he had benefited greatly by the cuttings made in the vegetable obstructions; his vessels, too, were without cargo, which facilitated their progress. They had with them a large herd of cattle, taken from some tribe during the voyage. The Baris flocked in great numbers to these new-comers, glad at the return of those who had formerly led them to plunder. They at once assisted them in the formation of their camp, although they had previously refused to do the same for the Government. Baker took an early opportunity of sending an official letter to Abou Saood, asking him, at the expiration of his contract, to withdraw all his people from the district under his command, and at the same time declaring the forfeiture to the Government of the cattle which had been stolen within his jurisdiction.

While this was pending, Abou Saood used his influence amongst Baker's own men to neutralize and damage the expedition, while he also fraternized with the Bari people. Unfortunately a scarcity of corn threatened them at the time, which helped to dispirit the troops. The crocodiles in the neighbourhood were exceedingly ferocious. Two sailors were carried off in two consecutive days, and a soldier had his leg smashed and shattered while bathing. Another sailor, while engaged in collecting the leaves of a kind of water convolvulus, which makes an excellent spinach, had his arm wrenched off at the elbow joint. A native woman, who had gone to the river to wash, was carried off. A necklace and two armlets, such as are worn by negro girls, were found in the stomach of a large crocodile shot by Baker afterwards, which proved that some one had been eaten and digested. The stomach also contained about five pounds weight of pebbles, which appeared to have been swallowed while feeding on flesh resting on the bank. 'The crocodile,' he writes, 'does not attempt to swallow an animal at once, but, retiring with it to some deep hole, tears it limb from limb with teeth and claws, devouring it at leisure.'

The detachment of men called the 'Forty Thieves' had been carefully drilled from the beginning of the expedition with most satisfactory results. They had become quite superior in morals and *régime* to the rest of the men. The Colonel, Abd-el-Kader, had so trained himself that he had become a capital shot. They were distinguished from the line regiment by a scarlet uniform, which was a simple red flannel shirt worn outside zouave trousers. They wore, besides, linen gaiters and a scarlet fez. All these men were thoroughly to be depended upon; in action they were always first; as skirmishers they proved invaluable, climbing rocks, pushing through jungles, and clearing the country of the enemy. They would not admit a thief into their ranks, and generally they became model soldiers. This led Baker to moralize on the fact that discipline such as is undergone by the common soldier, brought to bear on the ignorant savage, would be a rapid stride towards their future civilisation. It was also his opinion that, as the savage learns all he knows from his superiors, he would also quickly adopt their religious opinions.

They were still being constantly attacked, generally during the night, by those 'irrepressible vermin,' the Baris. Considering the people at the station fair game, they teased them like rats, sending out scouts in the darkness, who crawled upon hands and knees until within a few yards of the sentries. They then lie flat upon their bellies until they can retreat unobserved. The attacking force next approaches on hands and knees in perfect silence; they spring upon the sentries, and, with wild yells, make a general rush upon the camp. The Baris, combining with their enemies, the Lorquia, made a general attack on the camp on 21st July. They actually surprised the sentries; one corporal was killed, and a lieutenant and one soldier were wounded with arrows. The force at the station, in the excitement of the moment, had forgotten that they possessed artillery; so the natives were simply cowed and driven back by the firing of 1100 men, and their attempts at setting fire to the station were also frustrated by the thorn fence around it. This attack led to the construction of a ditch and earthwork, further to protect the station. During the month of August, the men began to complain of the scarcity of corn; they concluded that, if provisions fell short, this would oblige them to return to Khartoum. Abou Saood was also anxiously watching and waiting for their disappearance. Baker, in the meantime, concluded that he would begin an attack on Belinian during harvest time, by which means he would secure 2000 acres of *dhurra*, if the troops would work earnestly and secure it. On 30th August 1871, preparations were made for an attack on Belinian. There were about a hundred villages situated in the valley and along the base of the mountain at the latter place. An attack was made upon their stockades, and the natives were driven out of them. A number of fat calves and sheep were seized, and the stockades were fired. They next set about securing the corn, after appointing guards and sentries on all places exposed to attack. Baker's men, however, worked badly, because half-heartedly, in securing the corn, the natives working energetically during the night and carrying off ten times the amount gathered by the troops. Thousands of native women and children were engaged in boldly carrying it off. Baker heard at this time of the death of a missing major, Achmet Rafik. A herd of cattle was captured when making inquiries about the missing man. The natives, although routed, infested the plain, lying in the grass like snakes, and taking their revenge on any one who came near them. They could never tell where they were concealed; sometimes it was amongst the tall dhurra, behind bushes, and amongst the grass and scattered bush by the banks of the river. Ambuscades were appointed to clear the river and the country of them, and, being picked men from amongst the 'Forty Thieves,' they did their work well. After a short experience of them, the Baris were led to confess that it was useless to attempt to fight with such people, as the earth was full of soldiers, who sprang out of the ground beneath their feet. When the corn was conveyed to headquarters, they found it consisted only of about 670 bushels, while 650 men had been engaged in storing it. This would only last the troops two months on full rations, and a spirit of dissatisfaction began to spread amongst them. The men naturally disliked the object of the expedition, and would themselves have liked to have taken part in slave trading. They could not understand why the prisoners of war should not be held as slaves. On 13th October, the existence of a conspiracy amongst the officers to abandon the expedition was made known to Baker. This mutinous spirit was arrested by sudden orders being given to six companies of troops to push straight by river for the Bari islands, where abundance of corn was expected. There they indeed found abundance, with which they returned in triumph to Gondokoro. Another granary of corn was discovered farther southwards, but the natives keenly contested its possession. About 1100 people, comparatively useless to the expedition, including children, women, sailors, soldiers, and invalids, were sent down to Khartoum on 3d November. Amongst this number, in spite of orders to the contrary, many able-bodied men had been thus sent off; so that, exclusive of fifty-two sailors, the expedition was reduced to 502 officers and men. With this small force it seemed impossible to proceed to the interior. The Baris were still hostile; the traders were treacherous; the slave trade was to be suppressed with this handful of men, and territory in the equatorial districts was to be annexed. All this appeared to be favourable to the views of Abou Saood. Baker's term of service, too, would expire on 1st April 1873: there remained only one year and four months in which to accomplish his work. The Khedive was informed by letter of the conspiracy amongst the officers, and the necessity of opening the channel of the great White Nile was dwelt upon. Djiaffer Pasha at Khartoum was also communicated with for reinforcements and a supply of dhurra. Though thus reduced in numbers, the men were strong and healthy, and Baker determined to accomplish the mission he had undertaken.

On 10th November, Baker made a reconnaissance of the country at the last cataracts of the Nile, and about six miles south of their position. The high ground parallel to the river was found to be admirably suited for an agricultural settlement. They passed innumerable villages, with overflowing granaries. The population of the country was large, and the natives had proved themselves to be good agriculturists. Dhurra, sesamé, dochan, and beans are sown in oblongs and squares. They proved friendly, although of the Bari race. On the 13th November a herd of eleven bull-elephants was observed marching in close order along the bank of the river, totally unconscious of the near presence of enemies. Baker at once saddled his horse 'Greedy Grey,' taking rifles and ammunition with him. With the assistance of his men, these animals were surrounded, when they took to the water, which they crossed. While they were attempting to climb the steep bank on the opposite side, Baker shot two of them out of the eleven. The half-pounder rifles used were very deadly. 'They were certain,' he writes, 'to kill the elephant, and to half kill the man who fired them, with twelve drachms of fine-grain powder. I was tolerably strong, therefore I was never killed outright; but an Arab hunter had his collar-bone smashed by the recoil, when the rifle was loaded with simple coarse-grain powder. If he had used fine-grain, I should hardly have insured his life.' The bodies of the elephants floated two miles down stream, where they were secured. The natives of Bedden, flocking to the camp in hundreds, were delighted on receiving permission to take as much elephant's flesh as they required. Baker retained the two heads for his share of the spoil. The hostile Baris, watching the Baris of Bedden indulging to the full in elephant's flesh, could not resist the temptation. 'The temptation,' writes Baker, 'was too great to withstand. Who could resist flesh? The mouths of our enemies were watering as they watched the heavy loads of red meat carried upon the heads of the rival Baris. In the afternoon a messenger hailed the sentry, to say that one of the sheiks wished to present himself to me to crave a cessation of hostilities. Shortly after the disappearance of this man with a courteous answer, a batch of messengers arrived to beg that their chief might be received, as they all desired peace.' A general levee was held next morning. About twenty headmen of different villages had come to sue for peace. Peace was established with them, when the meeting concluded by a request for meat. This was granted them. This peace Baker concluded was the result of greediness and envy, as they had on previous occasions declined the offer of a large herd of cattle that would have been worth a hundred elephants. War had been brought on, wherein they had lost numbers of their people, and much corn, 'all of which they might have sold for cows; and they now desired peace, only to join in the scramble, like vultures, over the flesh of two elephants.' Perhaps this extraordinary craving for flesh may partly be accounted for from the fact that the Baris seldom kill their cattle. The cows are simply kept for their milk, and the bullocks to bleed. The cows are also bled at stated times, when the blood is boiled and eaten. Baker was able to bear out the testimony of Bruce, the traveller, as to the practice of cutting a steak from the hind-quarters of a living cow, as he had a fine bull with a hump which was similarly operated upon. The flesh is said to grow and fill up the vacancy caused by this operation.

Baker returned to Gondokoro highly satisfied with the results of the campaign. The magazines were filled with corn which would last them for a year; and peace had been established throughout the district, with a promise of assistance. The fear of the horses and the Snider rifles had spread throughout the country, the natives believing that no herds of cattle could escape the horses, and that the Snider rifles were magic. The nights at the station were now undisturbed. Baker now devoted his attention to all the necessary preparations for starting for the interior. Raouf Bey was to be left with a small force in charge of the station. The troops which had been under his personal command were very anxious to accompany him to the interior.

The detachment called the 'Forty Thieves' was in the meantime employed in making salt, which was collected in the neighbourhood of the station in a rough state and afterwards refined. The other natural productions of the place were: salts, iron, the oil-nut tree, and tamarinds in great abundance. When the cotton crop was ripe, the quality was found to be good, and he had it cleaned with a small hand-gin worked by two men.

Baker remarks that he had no time for elephant-shooting, else he might have killed a considerable number in the neighbourhood of Gondokoro. The Baris, not being good hunters, only attempt to take the elephant in pitfalls; so that, as it was seldom attacked, it was daring and easy of approach. The small ripe fruit of a tree called the heglik proved very attractive to them. Not unfrequently they would tear down the tree for the sake of the fruit, and even exert their strength against a huge tree by shaking it and afterwards gathering it up.

Baker arranged that he should be accompanied by 212 officers and men to the interior; and as they had been twelve months without communication with Khartoum, and their clothes were worn to rags, new scarlet flannel shirts and white trousers were dealt out to them. The number of men left at headquarters was 340, including 52 sailors. He was determined to penetrate into the south, carrying the steamer in sections, where she would be pieced together and launched on the river above the last cataracts, in order to open the communication with the Albert Nyanza. As large a supply of ammunition as possible was carried, in order to trade in ivory when they reached Unyoro or Magungo, Kamrasi's country.

The start was made from Gondokoro, or Ismailia, as Baker has named it, on 22d January 1872. For the first few days the men were in excellent spirits, and appeared to trust their leader. The vessels at times required to be towed round the sandbanks; this was done with great spirit by the men. An accident happening, which resulted in the death of one of the men, rather damped the spirits of the party at the outset. The foot of the cataracts was reached on 27th January; they found the spot very lovely, as the rocky islands were covered with rich green forest, in perpetual verdure. Bedden, the chief of that part of the country, came on board Baker's diahbeeah with some of his men, and professed to be quite willing to provide carriers to convey the baggage of the expedition farther southwards. It was agreed that the carriers should proceed as far as Loboré, about sixty miles from that place. Baker fully believed that he would be able to secure help here, and that they should be able to convey the carts, together with the steamer, to the navigable portion of the Nile in N. lat. 3° 32'.

Half of the cattle belonging to the expedition were offered to Bedden for this promised help. The conduct of the natives was now anything but reassuring, and several signs of distrust manifested themselves. No women or children came near the vessels, as they might be expected to do, and the cattle had all been driven away from the country. The cattle pens were found to be empty. At length Bedden condescended to return and say that his people had never previously acted as carriers for the Turks, nor would they now do so. The state of the White Nile had prevented all camel transport from Khartoum; and although cart and camel harness had been prepared, neither horse nor camel could be transported. The natives were so rich in dhurra and corn that they would not work; they were only ready to sleep or steal. There were about 2500 head of cattle and 1800 head of sheep in the camp, which were driven for safety to three small villages on the high sloping ground.   A night attack was made on this cattle kraal by the Baris, but they were ultimately repulsed.

Baker resolved, in his present paralyzed condition, that the Englishmen with the steamer sections must return to Gondokoro.   At the same time he determined to push on with one hundred men, in heavy marching order, to Loboré, where in all likelihood a sufficient number of porters could be secured to send back to the vessels, with an escort of fifty soldiers, in order to the advance southwards.   Major Abdullah was left in charge of the vessels with 120 men, a field-piece, and artillerymen, and the most careful precautions were taken for their safety in the case of an attack from the Baris. Lokko, an old rainmaker, joined Baker before the start was made, and the present of a cow's horn fitted with brass made him perfectly happy, and he proved a useful guide.   The start was made on 8th February, all the people being heavily laden. Mrs. Baker rode the horse called 'Greedy Grey,' which carried as much as could be hung upon the saddle.   Baker rode a powerful chestnut called 'Jamoos,' of Arab blood. Ten donkeys were laden with the officers' effects, spare ammunition, flour, etc.   Boxes were carried by twenty-two boatmen.   Colonel Abd-el-Kader and Captain Mohammed Deii were with the rear-guard, which drove 1000 cows and 5000 sheep.   The boys and girls, the personal servants of Mr. and Mrs. Baker, being remarkably obedient and well trained, all carried loads, and every one departed in good spirits after the check which had lately been imposed upon them.

The first halt was made at a village about three miles from the vessels.   There being plenty corn in the place, and the natives having deserted their habitations at their approach, they used the flour found in the village, and left two cows there by way of payment. Halting next at the village of Gobbohur, the natives brought a shell of 8¼ lbs., which had not been exploded, and which had been sold to them by the Baris of Belinian as a piece of iron. They hinted that they intended to hammer it into iron hoes, when they were warned that it would explode on being placed in the fire. Marengo was the next halting-place, on 10th February, the way that day being through lovely rocky scenery and fine park-like views. The rocks passed on the way consisted of syenite, gneiss, and large masses of white quartz.

Loboré was reached on 12th February, when a halt was made to await the cattle, which were some distance in the rear. Up till this time they had marched fifty-seven miles without firing a shot. Baker was glad to discover that the Loboré tribe had no connection with their recent troublesome neighbours the Bari. The old sheik, called Abbio, was half blind, but seemed willing to assist on hearing explanations, and granted a sufficient number of men to go back to the vessels as proposed, provided they were accompanied by the soldiers. A regular market was held shortly after their arrival for the purchase of flour in exchange for sheep and goats. Live goats were exchanged for about thirty pounds of flour, the weight of the one being about exactly equivalent to the weight of the other. The old sheik Abbio did indeed provide the requisite number of men as carriers to return and bring the stores from the vessels. As there was no doubt that the country farther southwards was greatly depopulated by the slave hunters, Baker took the precaution of securing 3740 lbs. of flour by 22d February. The ground in the neighbourhood of Loboré was like ' a beautiful park, characterized by numerous masses of granite, like ruined castles, among trees of all shades of green.' The antelopes and wild pigs which Baker bagged delighted the natives.

By 24th February the whole of the troops and baggage had arrived from the vessels ; all the arrangements made had been successful. They also brought tidings that the vessel had been attacked by the Baris after Baker's departure. There had been treachery on the part of the natives, and culpable negligence on the part of those in charge. The appearance of the four hundred men of the Loboré, with fifty soldiers in scarlet uniforms, had helped to decide the attack in favour of the troops. Five hundred natives were now engaged for the forward journey. Wani, the interpreter, an old acquaintance made on the former journey, superintended the arrangements necessary for collecting the carriers. The natives were allowed to select their own cattle by way of payment, and in doing so they proved rather fastidious. Baker found the Loboré great workers in iron, which was generally used for the manufacture of ornaments. They wore large rings of this metal round the neck, and upon the arms and ankles.

The start was again made on 29th February; the loads were prepared and arranged in divisions of twenty each, under the charge of selected officers. Unfortunately for the honesty of the Loboré, sixty-seven of the carriers had disappeared with as many cows, leaving only 433 for active service. These carriers were very powerful men, but careless and dishonest, and apparently wishing to seize an opportunity to escape on the road. After a halt was made, they would rush and scramble for their loads like wolves over a carcase, and in the process boxes and other et-ceteras were turned upside down quite heedlessly. An inverted canteen was discovered upon the head of one of these men, with the Cognac and gin showering down his body; he was, as Baker remarks, literally being basted with the liquor. Although these men were under a son of the sheik, his presence did not seem to do much in the way of preserving order.

In the onward march through a fine country of hills and low forest, they everywhere witnessed the desolating effect of the slave trade, passing large tracts of land which had formerly been under cultivation, and the charred remains of numerous villages. Abou Saood and his followers were responsible for these atrocities. They arrived at the spot where the Atabbi river joins the Asua. They waded through the latter, which was 120 yards in width. From a height of about a thousand feet above the Asua river, they enjoyed a splendid view of the entire landscape. A fine range of lofty hills, stretching in a long line towards Latooka, bordered their view to the east; on the west, on the left bank of the White Nile, was the precipitous mountain Neri. The river Nile here boils through the narrow gorge between the mountains. Continuing the journey, a magnificent view broke upon them. 'The grand White Nile,' he writes, 'lay like a broad streak of silver on our right, as it flowed in a calm deep stream direct from the Albert Nyanza, at this spot above all cataracts. No water had as yet been broken by a fall; the troubles of river life lay in the future; the journey to the sea might be said to have only just commenced. Here the entire volume flowed from the Albert Nyanza, distant hardly one degree; and here had I always hoped to bring my steamers, as the starting-point for the opening of the heart of Africa to navigation. I was deeply mortified when I gazed upon this lovely view, and reflected upon the impossibilities that had prevented my success. Had the White Nile been open as formerly, I should have trans-

ported the necessary camels from Khartoum, and there would
have been no serious difficulty in the delivery of the steamers
to this point.

'We now descended into the beautiful plain, to which I
had given the name of Ibrahimeyah, in honour of the father
of his Highness the Khedive (Ibrahim Pasha). This point
is destined to become the capital of Central Africa. The
general depot for the steamers will be near the mouth of
the Un-y-Amé river, which, after rising in the prairies between
Fatiko and Unyoro, winds through a lovely country for about
eighty miles, and falls into the White Nile opposite to Gebel
Kuka. The trade of Central Africa, when developed by the
steamers on the Albert Nyanza, will concentrate at this spot,
whence it must be conveyed by camels for 120 miles to Gondokoro, until at some future time a railway may perhaps continue
the line of steam communication.

'It is a curious fact that a short line of 120 miles of
railway would open up the very heart of Africa to steam
transport, between the Mediterranean and the equator, when
the line from Cairo to Khartoum shall be completed ! . . .

'I revelled in this lovely country. The fine park-like
trees were clumped in dark-green masses here and there.
The tall dolape palms were scattered about the plain, sometimes singly, at others growing in considerable numbers.
High and bold rocks ; near and distant mountains ; the richest
plain imaginable in the foreground, with the clear Un-y-Amé
flowing now in a shallow stream between its lofty banks, and
the grand old Nile upon our right—all combined to form a
landscape that produced a paradise. The air was delightful.
There was an elasticity of spirit, the result of a pure atmosphere,
that made one feel happy in spite of many anxieties. My

legs felt like steel as we strode along before the horses, with rifle on shoulder, into the broad valley, in which the mountain we had descended seemed to have taken root.'

The native name for this beautiful country was Afuddo, and they were now thirty-seven miles distant from Loboré. There were villages formerly around their present halting-place, but these had been destroyed by the slave-hunters. Baker now felt more at home, as the landscape presented many familiar features to him, and the mountain of Shooa, where he had camped for four or five months on his previous journey, was now distinctly visible. . They were now marching towards ko, one of Abou Saood's stations. Reaching the neigh- hood of the Shooa mountain, where the camp of Ibrahim en situated, and where he had formerly resided, they he place entirely destroyed. The whole way to Fatiko a most lovely route. The whole procession, headed by Baker, marched towards the slave station in the most orderly manner. Their appearance created confusion in the camp, immense numbers of slaves were driven out and hurried away to the south. Natives were seen rushing about armed with spears and shields. Two messengers approached them, one of them proving to be an old Cairo servant of Baker's. Abou Saood came out to meet them as they neared the station, in a humble, cringing attitude inviting them to some huts which had been prepared for their reception. Declining this invitation, Baker established his camp about a quarter of a mile beyond, beneath some large acacias. They were now 165 miles distant from Gondokoro.

The troops were reviewed, and a sham fight and attack on the Fatiko mountain was engaged in on 8th March. The natives appeared to be delighted at the sight, and assembled

in considerable numbers to witness it.   The music of the
band, produced by a number of bugles, drums, and cymbals,
together with a large military brass drum, had an overpowering
effect on them.   The natives proved themselves to be passion-
ately fond of music; and Baker hints that a London organ-
grinder might make a triumphal march through Central Africa,
followed by an admiring crowd, who would dance to the lively
tunes.   In the present instance, a crowd of naked Shooli
women, 'bounding about as musical enthusiasts,' began to
collect together, attracted by the band.   'Even the babies
were brought out to dance; and these infants, strapped to
their mothers' backs, and covered with pumpkin shells, like
young tortoises, were jolted about, without the slightest con-
sideration for the weakness of their necks, by their infatuated
mothers.   As usual among all tribes in Central Africa, the old
women were even more determined dancers than the young
girls.   Several old Venuses were making themselves extremely
ridiculous, as they sometimes do in civilised countries when
attempting the allurements of younger days.'   The men of the
Shooli and Fatiko tribes were the best proportioned Baker
had seen up till that time; they were muscular and well knit,
and generally their faces were handsome.   The women were
short of stature, but strong and compact, and walk about
perfectly naked.   The men, however, were partially clothed
with the skin of an antelope, slung across the shoulders and
covering the lower part of the body.

After these dancing performances were over, Baker was
visited by several of the natives, who related to him the
atrocities committed by Abou Saood's people.   The latter
had instigated the natives to attack them on their first appearance; but seeing Baker's powerful force, and perceiving in him

an old friend, they saw that this would be hopeless. The natives assured him that the whole country would rally round a good government—that what the people desired was protection and justice. Baker informed them, in return, that his intentions were peaceful, and that a recurrence of the atrocities committed by Abou Saood and his men would now be prevented. The traders' contract with the Soudan Government would expire in about twenty days, when Abou Saood would be obliged to retire, and the Government would be entirely in the hands of the Khedive. Baker had previously checked a conspiracy at Gondokoro, which had been instigated by Abou Saood, and now he had appeared at a moment when fortune was turning against them. The traders' people were discontented with their leaders, with their clothes and wages. Their parties had been massacred in several directions; about 500 loads of ivory, along with one of their stations, had been burned by a night attack of the Madi. Thirty-five of their party had been killed.

The news reached him here that Kamrasi, the former king of Unyoro, was dead; also that King Mtesa of Uganda had so far come under the personal influence of the traders from Zanzibar as to have become a Mohammedan. The throats of either man or beast were now cut in the name of God; he kept clerks, too, who could correspond in Arabic; and in addition to his other forces, he possessed a regiment armed with a thousand guns. Abou Saood had found Mtesa's people too strong for him; the traders of Zanzibar had been in the habit of dealing with them, and purchasing ivory from Mtesa with cotton stuffs, silks, guns, powder, beads, etc. The commodities of Zanzibar were not uncommon at Fatiko. Abou Saood's slave-hunters received a terrible blow from the Umiro

tribe. Ali Hussein, a villainous Arab who had made a
successful attack upon them once, determined again to proceed
against them. The Umiros had, however, laid an ambuscade,
which resulted in the massacre of 103 of Abou Saood's men,
and about 150 of their allies. This spread a panic amongst
the slave-hunters, who returned to Fatiko broken and
unsuccessful. Mahommed Wat-el-Mek, the son of a small
king on the Blue Nile, was one of the most energetic and
adventurous of the slave-hunters, now under Abou Saood;
every nook and corner of the country was known to him.
While occupying the station at Faloro, he had been hospitable
to Speke and Grant on their arrival from Zanzibar. Speke, on
parting from him at Gondokoro, had presented him with a
beautiful double-barrelled rifle and several other articles.
Baker was anxious that this man's services should be secured
and added to his company.

Baker issued orders that the sneaking villain Abou Saood
should cease his slave-hunting operations immediately his
contract had expired. He was only to remain on sufferance
in the country, and until his ivory had been removed to
Gondokoro. The different stations at Fabbo, Farragenia, it
was well known, were crowded with slaves; but with these
Baker did not intend to interfere. It was arranged that a
Government officer, with a detachment of 100 men, should
be stationed near Fatiko, as a watch upon their movements.
This station was within a hundred yards of the south extremity
of that of Abou Saood.

The sheik of the district of Fatiko, in the country of Shooli,
appeared in person on a visit to Baker on 16th March. This
great man was perfectly smeared with red ochre and grease
from head to foot; a well-dressed skin of an antelope was

slung across his shoulder, and descended across his loins. He expressed himself very bitterly during the interview against the slave-traders, and offered his allegiance to the Khedive. He was assured that he had nothing to fear from the slave-traders in future. Baker gave him several presents, and, according to his usual custom, the seeds of the best Egyptian cotton, tomatoes, pumpkins, cucumbers, water-melons, sweet-melons, barmian, maize, etc. A close acquaintance with the magnetic battery surprised and delighted him.

Leaving Major Abdullah in charge of the station, the expedition started southwards towards Unyoro. The limit of the inhabited country stretched but three miles beyond the camp at Fatiko; the remainder of the way was wilderness to Unyoro. They reached the banks of the Victoria Nile on 22d March, where the river flowed beneath cliffs of seventy or eighty feet in depth through magnificent forest. They halted on the day following exactly opposite one of Abou Saood's stations, under the command of a man named Suleiman. 'It is impossible,' he writes, 'to describe the change that has taken place since I last visited this country. It was then a perfect garden, thickly populated, and producing all that man could desire. The villages were numerous; groves of plantains fringed the steep cliffs on the river's bank; and the natives were neatly dressed in the bark cloth of the country. The scene has changed! All is wilderness! The population has fled! Not a village is to be seen! This is the certain result of the settlement of Khartoum traders. They kidnap the women and children for slaves, and plunder and destroy wherever they set their foot.' Baker found that Abou Saood had given no intimation to his agent Suleiman of the expiration of his contract. The new king, successor to Kamrasi, was Kabba Réga, to whom Baker made known his mission, and sent him many substantial presents. An official message was also sent to Suleiman, telling him 'that sixteen days hence the contract would expire, and that he and all his people must be ready to evacuate the country and return to Khartoum on that day. That any person who should remain after this notice would be imprisoned. That, should he or any of his people wish to enlist in the service of the Government as irregular troops, their names must be handed in before the expiration of two days.' Sixty-one men registered their names under Baker. Kabba Réga, like his father Kamrasi, kept Baker waiting a long time for a reply; and in the meantime his cattle were dying every day, and provisions were only coming in in small quantities. They were obliged to subsist mostly on vegetable food. The rain came down nearly every day. Had he not been provided with cattle, they would have been half-starved, as nothing was procurable save beans, sweet potatoes, and plantains.

The order was given on 8th April, by Kabba Réga, that Baker was to be supplied with carriers for the journey to Masindi. The start was at last made from Foweera; the march was through forest and grass about four feet high, until Kisoona, a poor straggling place in the centre of the forest, was reached. The neighbourhood was populous, but the villages were all concealed in the forest amidst groves of bananas. Next morning, the 12th of April, it was found that 200 carriers had absconded. Colonel Abd-el-Kader was at once sent back to Foweera with a letter to Suleiman, asking him to collect 300 men at once to return with the effects to the latter place. Abd-el-Kader found that Suleiman had acted in a treacherous manner, and that his people had been allowed to escape with all their slaves and effects. The greater number of Suleiman's people had escaped to Fabbo. Suleiman and Eddrees were captured and tried before Baker. The charges against Suleiman were all clearly proven. He had conspired to attack Rionga in opposition to Baker's orders; had spoken treasonably against the Government; had arranged and abetted the escape of the new levy which had joined the Government service, with the slaves; he had also murdered with his own hand a native confided to his care. As a first instalment of future punishment, 200 lashes were inflicted upon him on the spot, while his accomplice Eddrees received 100 lashes. The native chiefs bore witness that Suleiman was the chief offender; that he had ruined the country, kidnapping the women and children; and that, as a result, the natives had fled from their homes. The chiefs who were witnesses of the trial expressed their confidence in the Government.

On the march to Masindi they encountered Kittakara, a kind of prime minister to Kabba Réga, who treated them courteously, and never asked for presents. There was still an impression of general ruin throughout the country when they halted at Chosrobeze, in lat. 1° 57′ N. The traders had ransacked the district for slaves, with the usual result.

Masindi, the capital of Unyoro, was reached on 25th April. The town was composed of about a thousand large beehive-shaped straw huts, without any arrangement or plan, and is situated on high undulating land, with a wide view. The country around is open, and is covered with high grass. Having selected a position beneath a large banian tree, they proceeded to form the encampment. Kabba Réga, the young king, sent them presents of provisions. The spot where they had encamped was seventy-nine miles from the river at

Foweera, and three hundred and twenty-two miles by route from Ismailia or Gondokoro.

An official visit was made to Kabba Réga on 26th April. They found the young king sitting in his divan, which was a large newly-constructed hut, ornamented with some common printed cotton cloths from Zanzibar. He was clad in bark-cloth striped with black, beautifully made. He appeared to be about twenty years of age. Baker explained to him the intentions of the Khedive of Egypt regarding the slave trade, and expressed his regret at the state in which he now found the country. The prisoners who had been captured by Colonel Abd-el-Kader were publicly flogged in the presence of the people, and Suleiman and Eddrees were led away in chains. The slaves belonging to Unyoro found in their possession were then liberated. Kabba Réga returned Baker's visit on 27th April, but it was plain that he was full of suspicions, and that he was trembling with nervous anxiety. A crowd of about 2000 people had accompanied him, making a tremendous din with whistles, horns, and drums. He was closely accompanied by four of his great chiefs. Amongst the crowd following him were the sorcerers; they were curiously dressed, having fictitious beards, manufactured from a number of bushy cows' tails. Baker has given a capital full-length portrait of Kabba Réga, which we quote:—

'Kabba Réga was about five feet ten inches in height, and of extremely light complexion. His eyes were very large, but projected in a disagreeable manner. A broad but low forehead and high cheek-bones, added to a large mouth, with rather prominent but exceedingly white teeth, complete the description of his face. His hands were beautifully shaped, and his finger-nails were carefully pared and scrupulously clean. The nails of his feet were equally well attended to. He wore sandals of raw buffalo hide, but neatly formed, and turned up round the edges. His robe of bark-cloth, which completely covered his body, was exquisitely made, and had been manufactured in Uganda, which country is celebrated for this curious production.' This was Kabba Réga, the son of Kamrasi, the sixteenth king of Unyoro, of the Galla conquerors, a *gauche*, awkward, undignified lout of twenty years of age, who thought himself a great monarch. He was cowardly, cruel, cunning, and treacherous to the last degree. Not only had he ordered the destruction of his brother, Kabka Miro, but, after his death, he had invited all his principal relations to visit him; these he had received with the greatest kindness, and, at parting, he had presented them with gifts, together with an escort of his body-guard, called *barasoora*, to see them safe home. These men, by the young king's instructions, murdered them all in the high grass during their return journey. By these means he had got rid of troublesome relations, and he now sat secure upon the throne with only one great enemy; this was Rionga, the staunch and determined foe of his father, who had escaped from every treachery, and still lived to defy him in the north-eastern provinces of Unyoro.

Of course one of Kabba Réga's first requests was Baker's assistance in order to capture and kill Rionga. His mind was only diverted from this request by a display of the presents which had been brought for his father, Kamrasi. Being the son of his father, he at once demanded that all the presents intended for his father should be bestowed upon himself. The importance of regular commerce and the establishment of proper communication by a regular route from the north was dwelt upon by Baker. The whole of the equatorial Nile basin was now to be taken under the protection of the Khedive. No unnecessary wars would be permitted, and he, Kabba Réga, might remain as the representative of the Government. He was assured that no country could prosper without industry and good government, that agriculture was the foundation of a country's wealth, and that war, being a disturbing element, helped to ruin the country. This led Kabba Réga to speak of his favourite grievance, that 'Rionga was the sole cause of war, therefore it would be necessary to destroy him before any improvements could be made. If Rionga were killed, and the slave-hunters expelled from the country, there might be some hope of progress; but that it was wasting breath to talk of commerce and agriculture until Rionga should be destroyed.' This was much to the same tune as the continual speeches made by his father, from all of which Baker concluded that Rionga must be a very fine fellow, and much superior to either Kamrasi or his son. No argument was of any avail, and Kabba Réga continued to clamour for help to fight against Rionga.

Traces of the presence and of the treachery of Abou Saood were soon self-evident. He had arrived at Masindi in a very dirty and miserable condition, and riding on a donkey. He spread the report that the Pasha was a very different person from the traveller who had formerly been in the country, and that the first mentioned was dead. 'The Pasha,' said Abou Saood, 'is not like the traveller, or any other man. He is a monster with three separate heads, in each of which are six eyes, three upon each side. Thus, with eighteen eyes, he can see everything and every country at once. He has three enormous mouths, which are furnished with teeth like those of a crocodile, and he devours human flesh. He has already killed and eaten the Bari people, and destroyed their country. Should he arrive here, he will pull you from the throne and seize your kingdom. You must fight him, and by no means allow him to cross the river at Foweera. My soldiers will fight him on the road from Gondokoro, as will all the natives of the country; but I don't think he will be able to leave Gondokoro, as he has a large amount of baggage, and I have told the Baris not to transport it. Thus he will have no carriers.' At this absurd picture of himself Baker laughed outright, but felt that all this was quite consistent with the treacherous part he had always acted.

Baker began the formation of a garden around the camp, employing the prisoners in clearing the grass, while the soldiers began the work of cultivation with native hoes. The building of a government house and public divan was commenced on 29th April. Umbogo, the interpreter, having come to the conclusion that the reason of the difference between white men and black was that the former was, in the habit of using soap, while the latter did not, a piece of soap was given him by Baker, which pleased him immensely. Terrible stories of the atrocities of slavers were told to him. Throughout Unyoro, in troublous times, the corn is not kept in exposed granaries, but buried in the ground in deep holes. When these slave-hunters were in search of corn, they would catch one of the villagers, and holding the captive over a large jar filled with glowing embers, would roast his posteriors in order to make him tell where the corn was hidden. If this did not extract the secret, then the throat of the victim was cut as a warning to the rest.

The experience of our traveller, gathered from every native

tribe amongst which he dwelt, was that slavery was a natural institution of the country, only their reading of the eighth commandment was, 'Thou shalt not steal from me.' Although Kabba Réga and his people had no objection to the restoration of the slaves which had been stolen from Unyoro, they still continued the practice of slave-dealing amongst themselves. The value of a healthy young girl in Unyoro was equal to a single elephant's tusk of the first class, or to a new shirt. In Uganda, where needles were in great demand, a handsome girl might be purchased for thirteen English needles. On the year of his arrival at Gondokoro, Baker had a very interesting conversation with a sheik of the Shir tribe on the subject of the slave trade. Many of his tribe had been kidnapped by neighbouring people, and he wished Baker to organize an expedition against them. In the course of the conversation he seemed moved at the allusion to the forcible separation of children from their parents.

' Have you a son?' he asked.

' My sons are unfortunately dead,' replied Baker.

' Indeed!' he exclaimed. ' I have a son—an only son. He is a nice boy—a very good boy; about so high (showing his length upon the handle of his spear). I should like you to see my boy. He is very thin now; but if he should remain with you he would soon get fat. He's a really nice boy, and *always hungry.* You'll be so fond of him; he'll eat from morning till night, and still he'll be hungry. You'll like him amazingly; he'll give you no trouble if you only give him plenty to eat. He'll lie down and go to sleep, and he'll wake up hungry again. He's a good boy indeed; and he's my only son. I'll sell him to you for a molote!' (native iron spade). This is certainly a shocking story, but one which becomes a reality often enough, in seasons of scarcity, amongst the White Nile tribes.

The only way in which girls are disposed of is by purchase as wives, each daughter in a family selling for twelve or fifteen cows to her suitor. In Unyoro, owing to the scarcity of cows, the girls are bought for such commodities as brass-coil bracelets, bark-cloths, cotton shirts, ivory, etc.

The Government House, as it was called, consisted of a building containing only one room twenty-eight feet long by fourteen wide, and about twenty feet high. It was carefully thatched, and had a commodious porch; the inside walls were neatly made with canes closely lashed together. This was the divan or public room, but a back door communicated by a covered way to Baker's private residence. The private room was twenty-four feet long by thirteen wide, was arranged as neatly as possible, in order to excite the admiration of the people and make them familiar with the manners and customs of more civilised life, which it was to be hoped they might imitate, and also improve trade. ' The walls,' he writes, ' were as usual made of canes, but these were carefully hung with scarlet blankets, sewn together and stretched to the ground, so as to form an even surface. The floor was covered with mats. Upon the walls opposite to each other, so as to throw endless reflections, were two large oval mirrors (girandoles) in gilt metal frames. A photograph of Her Majesty the Queen stood on the toilet table. At the extreme end of the room was a very good coloured print, nearly life size, of Her Royal Highness the Princess of Wales. The scarlet walls were hung with large coloured prints, life size, of very beautiful women, with very gorgeous dresses, all the jewellery being imitated by pieces of coloured tinsel. A

number of sporting prints, very large, and also coloured, were
arranged in convenient places on the walls.   There were fox-
hunting scenes, and German stag-hunts, together with a few
quiet landscapes, that always recalled the dear old country
now so far away.   The furniture was simple enough ; two
angarebs, or Arab stretchers, which during the day were
covered with Persian carpets and served as sofas, while at
night they were arranged as beds.   The tables were made of
square metal boxes piled one upon the other, and covered
with bright blue cloths.   These were arranged with all kinds
of odd trinkets of gaudy appearance, but of little value, which
were intended to be asked for, and given away.   Two native
stools curiously cut out of a solid block formed our chairs.
The guns and rifles stood in a row against a rack covered
with red Turkey cloth ; and a large Geneva musical box lay
upon a table beneath the Princess of Wales.

This room, as a matter of course, soon became the wonder
of the place.   When Kabba Réga honoured this curiosity-
shop with his presence on the 11th May, the first thing he
said was, ' Are these all for me ? '   ' Certainly,' replied Baker,
' if you wish to exchange ivory.   All these things belong to
the Khedive of Egypt, and any amount remains in the
magazines at Gondokoro.   These are simply a few curiosities
that I have brought as an experiment to prove the possibility
of establishing a trade.'   The wheel of life attracted much
attention, neither Kabba Réga nor any of his chiefs ever tiring
of the display.   Each of the chiefs had in turn to submit to
the magnetic battery, and Kabba Réga was not a little amused
to witness a favourite minister rolling on his back in con-
tortions.   The large looking-glasses were miracles, and they
set them down as ' cojoor ' (magic).   Amongst the pictures

of gaily - dressed female figures, they had the good taste to select the picture of the Princess of Wales as the most lovely. One thing Kabba Réga could not understand was, 'why the women in the various portraits all looked at him.' Wherever he moved, their eyes always seemed to follow him. This made the chiefs also feel uncomfortable. In examining the guns and rifles, Kabba Réga inquired which of them were intended for him. His uncle Rabouka also remarked to Baker that he had done wisely in bringing all these guns as presents for Kabba Réga. About the musical box the remark was made that the latter 'might set this going at night to play you to sleep, when you were too drunk to play an instrument yourself, even if you knew how to do it.' On being refused several articles, the personal belongings of Lady Baker, he peevishly exclaimed, 'Everything that is worth having seems to belong to *the Sit*' (the lady).

The ceremony of the official annexation of Unyoro in the name of the Khedive of Egypt was performed on the 14th of May 1872. As a proof of his satisfaction with this arrangement, the young king sent Baker a present of twelve goats.

On 23d May a party was sent off to Fatiko, with letters to be forwarded to Egypt, Khartoum, and England, and also with written instructions to Major Abdullah to arrest Abou Saood, who had, contrary to orders, defied Baker's authority and kidnapped slaves in Unyoro since his contract had expired. He was to be taken prisoner and delivered up to Raouf Bey at Gondokoro, while he was to march himself, together with the liberated slaves, to Foweera.

A brisk and hopeful trade was now inaugurated. Ivory was being received in exchange for different commodities, at a profit to the Government, when realized, of between 1500 and

2000 per cent. A few beads, three or four coloured cotton handkerchiefs, a zinc mirror, and a fourpenny butcher's knife, would purchase a tusk of ivory worth between twenty and thirty pounds. Baker remarks in regard to these transactions, that at the conclusion of a bargain in Unyoro each party thought he had the best of it. The young king, however, interdicted this system of free trade so auspiciously begun, and ordered that all the tusks for sale should be brought to him. The climate of Masindi had proved excellent for the agricultural experiments; the produce sown proved very thriving. The air was always fresh and invigorating, as they were 4000 feet above the sea level; the Unyoro people, however, spent the day in sleep or idleness, unconscious of their privileges. Ramadan, clerk of the detachment, was appointed by Baker to start a school, as he had mastered sufficient of the Unyoro language to make them understand, and as it would be well to bestow upon them the blessings of education as well as of commerce. An incident occurred on the 31st May which filled the explorer's mind with ominous suspicions. While the troops were being put through their musketry drill, they were suddenly surrounded by five or six thousand men, armed with spears and shields, and all in a state of frantic excitement. The order was immediately given to form in square, which puzzled the natives extremely. By putting a bold front on the matter, and appearing only to be amused, the rising was averted and bloodshed prevented.

As the miserable young king, Kabba Réga, spent most of his time in a state of semi-intoxication, and as they were liable at any moment to the infliction of any foolish order he might issue, and as he was also offended, in self-defence Baker built a fort for greater security. This fort was finished in a few days, so that they had an impregnable protection in a position nearly half-way between the entrance of the main approach and the Government house.

Envoys were received direct from King Mtesa of Uganda, on 4th June, bearing a letter of welcome for Baker, written in Arabic. These men were well dressed in Indian clothes, and to our traveller appeared quite civilised, as though native merchants of Bombay. Presents were bestowed upon them, for which they were duly grateful. In reply to inquiries made, nothing had been heard of Livingstone. Baker wrote a letter to Mtesa, asking him to use every endeavour to find the great traveller, and send him on to Masindi. Two letters were also written for the great traveller, which were consigned to Mtesa's care. Baker's letter to Mtesa complimented him upon the general improvement of his country, upon his conversion from heathenism, and described the object of the expedition as one intended to open up a trade from the north that would bring merchandise of every description into the kingdom. Baker here advised him to send his own carriers, as Kabba Réga was jealous, and would endeavour to monopolize the trade. The envoys returned to Uganda, with the tidings of Speke's death, and much gratified by all they had seen.

Towards the beginning of June, Kabba Réga began to stint them of their provisions, and on the 7th there was really nothing for the troops to eat. Matouse, a tall chief, brought a present of seven jars of plantain cider and two large packages of flour, which he asserted he had borrowed from Rabouka, promising more corn on the following day. The cider was distributed amongst the soldiers, and many of them partook of it. After dinner, Abd-el-Kader made his appearance at the divan in a state of great excitement, saying that 'many of the troops appeared to be dying, and they had evidently been poisoned by the plantain cider.' Baker appealed at once to his medicine-chest, supplying himself with tartar-emetic, mustard, and salt and water. On arriving at the camp, which was some little distance away, he found the men in a terrible state. Several of them were lying insensible, while about thirty suffered from violent constriction of the throat, which almost stopped their breathing. Each man was dosed with tartar-emetic, and afterwards with mustard and salt and water, and by next morning the danger was past.

Suspecting a treacherous attack, the sentries were doubled, and Matouse, the chief who had sent the cider, was requested to come over to the Government house. The message was sent that he would come over on the following day. An ominous silence seemed to reign over the village of Masindi that night. On the following morning quite an unexpected attack was made upon them ; shots were fired from behind the bushes surrounding the station, and the sergeant who followed Baker, as he moved towards the divan for his rifle, fell, shot through the heart. The bugle was sounded without a moment's delay, and the troops fell into position around the station, and were soon pouring a heavy fire into the grass around the station where the enemy lay concealed. Those in ambush in front of the station were quickly driven out by a heavy fire from the 'Forty Thieves.' Blue lights were soon in requisition, and Kabba Réga's large divan, as well as a number of the straw dwellings around, were set on fire. The young cowardly king had fled, with all his women, before the action commenced.

Moving forward under cover of the terrible conflagration of the town, the enemy was met wherever they made a stand.

'The blue lights,' writes Baker, 'continued the work of vengeance; the roar of flames and the dense volumes of smoke, mingled with the continued rattle of musketry and the savage yells of the natives, swept forward with the breeze, and the capital of Unyoro was a fair sample of the infernal regions. The natives were driven out of the town, but the high grass was swarming with many thousands.' A steady fire of Snider rifles soon cleared the grass, and in one hour and a quarter the battle of Masindi was won. All that remained of the formerly extensive town was a vast open space of smoke and black ashes. The enemy had fled.

After ordering the bugle to cease firing, Baker found that he had lost four men; one of them was a faithful, devoted, and unselfish officer, Monsoor. After burying these men decently near the fort, with a heavy heart Baker wrote these words in his journal: 'Thus ended the battle of Masindi, caused by the horrible treachery of the natives. Had I not been quick in sounding the bugle and immediately assuming a vigorous offensive, we should have been overwhelmed by numbers. Since we have been in this country, my men have been models of virtue; nothing has been stolen, except a few potatoes on one occasion, when the thief was publicly punished, and the potatoes restored to the owner; neither have the natives been interfered with in any manner. I have driven the slave-hunters from their country, and my troops from Fatiko are ordered to restore to Unyoro all the slaves that have been stolen by the traders. The disgusting ingratitude and treachery of the negro surpasses imagination. What is to become of these countries? All my good-will brings forth evil deeds.' Baker was, however, eminently well satisfied with the demeanour of his officers and men when the station was attacked by the seven or eight thousand natives. Nothing, he writes, could have exceeded their cool, soldier-like bearing. In walking unarmed over the burnt town, Baker narrowly missed being speared by a treacherous native.

Baker determined that if hostilities should continue, he would proclaim Rionga, the enemy of Kabba Réga, as the representative of the Government, as vassal-chief in Unyoro. As there was no possible means of communication with Abdullah, who had been left in charge of the station at Fatiko, in case of necessity it was decided that a march should be made to the Victoria Nile in order to meet and form an alliance with Rionga.

Kabba Réga, from a distance, pretended to sue for peace, but all his proposals were blown to the winds by a continuance of treacherous conduct. The abandoned quarters in the neighbourhood of the fort were fired. On the 13th June a sudden rush of natives was made upon the cattle, which were grazing within a short distance of the fort, poisoned arrows were thrown, and guns fired into the camp. The natives were, however, speedily driven from the high grass around the station. Orders were given for the destruction of all the villages in the neighbourhood, as no doubt remained that Kabba Réga's intention was to massacre all at the station.

Baker collected his forces, and addressing them, arranged the plan of march to Foweera, from whence they would reach Rionga. 'A Bari, who professed to know the path, would lead the advance-guard of fifteen Sniders, commanded by Lieutenant-Colonel Abd-el-Kader, supported by myself with ten Sniders in charge of the ammunition, accompanied by Lieutenant Baker, my wife, and two servants, carrying double breech-loading elephant rifles. The rear-guard would consist

of fifteen Sniders.' Orders were given as to the plan of march
and how to comport themselves in case of attack. The
baggage that could be carried was divided into the requisite
amount of loads. When this was accomplished, the remainder
of the baggage was arranged in piles in the Government house,
was soaked with nitrous ether, spirits of wine, lamp-oil, spirits
of turpentine; the building was then fired, and the whole rose
in flames.

The march from Masindi to Foweera was begun on the
14th June 1872. They arrived at the latter place, after
innumerable perils and hardships, on the 24th June. Nothing
remained but blackened ashes of the old station. In the
dangerous march of about eighty miles, his losses had been ten
men killed and eleven wounded. An enormous quantity of
ammunition had been used on the way, which was lined with
ambuscades of Kabba Réga's people.

Rionga's quarters were reached on 18th July, when Baker
received a warm welcome. Presents had been exchanged:
those from Rionga were a cow, sheep, and a load of corn;
Baker had given him a beautiful cloak of gold brocade,
together with a new tarboosh and sky-blue turban. 'He was,'
we are told, 'a handsome man of about fifty, with exceedingly
good manners. He had none of the stiffness of Kamrasi, nor
the *gauche* bearing of Kabba Réga, but he was perfectly at his
ease.' He was well aware of all that had taken place at
Masindi, and he declared that Abou Saood had long ago
arranged a plan with Kabba Réga for his destruction. Rionga
was well aware of how Baker had refused to attack him; he
promised to remain a faithful representative of the Khedive's
Government. The ceremony of blood brotherhood was gone
through, and an entertainment was held in honour of his

arrival. Baker speedily made friends with these tribes; the bestowal of a few red and yellow handkerchiefs and two or three pounds of red and white beads was sufficient. Rionga was proclaimed agent of the Government, who would rule Unyoro in place of Kabba Réga, deposed. Leaving sixty-five men in a powerful stockade which he had constructed, Baker started with forty men to the station at Fatiko, in order to inquire as to what had happened in his absence. This place was reached on 2d August, much to the relief of Major Abdullah. No one came to greet the party from Abou Saood's station, which Baker took as a studied insult. A review of the troops was gone through, when the slavers' men gathered in a suspicious attitude some little distance away. Wat-el-Mek, their leader, was summoned to appear before Baker, but he refused. Very shortly the slavers' men began firing on the Government troops, and seven men were struck within a few seconds. The enemy kept at a distance of about ninety yards away, and fired in a kneeling posture, when they retired behind the huts to reload. They thus kept up a hot fire. Baker ordered the bugler to sound 'Charge bayonets,' and led his men against them. The slavers' men immediately took to flight. Wat-el-Mek, in attempting to shoot Baker, had one of his fingers cut off and his gun halved in two by a shot from the 'Dutchman,' which he always carried. They were pursued for four miles. A herd of 306 cattle, 130 slaves, 15 donkeys, 43 prisoners, 7 flags, and the entire station were thus captured from the enemy.

The enemy had more than half their number killed. On asking where one of the leaders, Ali Hussein, was, 'Dead!' cried a number of voices.

'Are you certain?' Baker asked.

'We will bring you his head, for he is not far off,' they replied; and several men started immediately.

Breakfast was hardly concluded, when some natives rushed in and threw the head of Ali Hussein on the floor of the hut. This noted slave-hunter had been alive when he was discovered, but was quickly despatched.

Baker was obliged to attend personally on the seven wounded men, owing to the fact of his having no medical officer at hand. On the 3d August, evidence was given against Abou Saood by Mahommed Wat-el-Mek and another prisoner, both swearing on the Koran that they had only obeyed his orders in attacking the troops. Wat-el-Mek soon afterwards joined the Government troops, and behaved well from that time. Suleiman, another of the ringleaders, was pardoned and reinstated, being made vakeel of the Fabbo station, under the command of Wat-el-Mek. All the evidence which could be brought forward was to the effect that all the opposition which he had hitherto met with had been caused by Abou Saood. The latter escaped to Khartoum, and thence to Cairo, after a *lying* interview with Baker, and spread all manner of evil reports regarding him.

Another attempt was made by Abou Saood's slave-hunters to secure the three thousand tusks of ivory which had been confiscated to the Government at Fabbo station. In this they were entirely unsuccessful, as the three thousand Makkarika cannibals who had been enlisted in the cause heard the real truth regarding the difficulties of the work. 'Fight the Pasha!' the spies had exclaimed; 'do you not know who he is? and that he could kill you all like fowls, as he did the people of Ali Hussein? He has no cows for you to carry off, but he has guns that are magic, and which load from behind instead of at the muzzle!' News arrived that Rionga, in company with some other tribes, had defeated Kabba Réga, and that he was in hiding on the borders of the Albert Nyanza. Mtesa, king of Uganda, had also invaded Unyoro from the south, and had sent six thousand men under his general, Congow, to be placed at Baker's disposal. Mtesa had heard with rage and dismay of the destruction of the goods at the station at Masindi, which had been intended for himself. The fort of Fatiko, which had been commenced on the 28th August, was finished on the 25th December, and only awaited the reinforcements which had been sent for from Gondokoro. The natives in the district paid the corn-tax demanded of them with great good-humour.

The time passed happily at Fatiko. A vast hunt was organized, when about a mile and a half of the prairie land was netted, the grass fired to windward, and the game thus driven towards the nets was speared and shot by those in ambush. The natives acknowledged several clearly-defined laws in the pursuit of game. The natives were very dexterous in the use of the simple hunting spear, but accidents were frequent in fighting with the wounded animals. As the game was abundant around the station, the troops were kept well supplied, and large quantities were given to the natives. A lioness having been shot in the grass after a desperate encounter, a meeting of the women was held in Gimoro's village, when the following was the report of what was passed. The conclusion these women had arrived at was, 'that the Pasha must not be allowed to go out hunting, as he might possibly be killed by a lion or a buffalo. What would happen to us if any accident should befall our father? Would not the slave - hunters immediately return to the country and destroy us, simply because he had protected us? Do we not now sleep in peace? and were we not always awake at night before he came among us?' Baker terms them excellent people, and well cared for by the men; but the ladies' declaration regarding himself he could scarcely call *petticoat* government, as they were entirely without attire of the latter sort.

'My fort at Fatiko was within call of two large villages—those of Gomoro and the sheik of the country. During my sojourn of seven months, I never heard a woman scream, neither was there any domestic or civil disturbance. There were no police required in that country. There were no pickpockets, as there were no pockets to pick, which was one advantage in favour of nudity. A London police magistrate would have died of *ennui;* the constables could not even have sworn to a case of intoxication, merely as a matter of form to afford him employment. There were no immoral females to disgrace the public streets; neither were there any beggars, vagrants, organ-grinders, or perambulators, to worry, deafen, or upset you. My country was a picture of true harmony. We had no complex machinery of law; there was no such difficulty as an estate in Chancery; no divorce court, or cases of *crim. con.* that necessitated an appeal. . . . I had no ecclesiastical difficulties. . . . My troops were Mohammedans, without an opposing sect; therefore, for lack of opposition, they were lukewarm believers. The natives believed in nothing. The curious fact remained, that without the slightest principle of worship, or even a natural religious instinct, these people should be free from many vices that disgrace a civilised community. I endeavoured to persuade the most intelligent of the existence of a Deity who could reward or punish; but beyond this I dared not venture, as they would have asked practical questions, which I could not have explained to their material understanding.'

Baker accounted for the great mortality which existed amongst all infants, from two years old to five, by the absurd custom of public night nurseries. Certain houses were built upon stone supports, about three feet from the ground. In the clay wall of the circular building is a round hole about a foot in diameter, this being the only aperture. 'At sunset,' he writes, 'when the children have been fed, they are put to bed in the simplest manner, by being thrust head foremost through the hole in the wall, assisted, if refractory, by a smack behind, until the night nursery shall have received the limited number. The aperture is then stopped up with a bundle of grass if the nights are cool. The children lie together on the clay floor like a litter of young puppies, and breathe the foulest air until morning, at which time they are released from the suffocating oven, to be suddenly exposed to the chilly daybreak. Their naked little bodies shiver round a fire until the sun warms them; but the seeds of diarrhœa and dysentery have already been sown.'

Envoys arrived from King Mtesa of Uganda on 15th January 1873, with a friendly letter, and telling of the army which he had sent Baker on the news of Kabba Réga's treachery. The king requested that he should visit him. There was no news of Livingstone, but the two letters sent addressed to him had been forwarded in different directions. Fresh envoys arrived on 11th February with another letter, and the road was declared to be practically open between Fatiko and Zanzibar through his friendship. These envoys returned on 13th February with a representative from Baker, and a letter to Livingstone. Mtesa not only delivered this letter to Lieutenant Cameron, R.N., at Unyanyembe, but actually sent his reply to Baker. The latter asked him to recall his troops from Unyoro, thanked him heartily for his interest and kindness, and sent him a few presents.

The expected reinforcements arrived from Gondokoro on 8th March. Great delays had been experienced on their journey, having been thirteen months on the way from Khartoum. Having now six hundred and twenty men, the stations of Fatiko, Fabbo, and Taniodoli, the stockades opposite Rionga's island, were strongly garrisoned. Clear and explicit orders were written out for the use of Major Abdullah, who was left in charge of the station at Fatiko, and Baker was ready to start for Gondokoro on 20th March. Having been two years and five months without any communication from Egypt or Europe, about six hundred copies of the *Times* had arrived at once.

The expedition arrived in good order at Gondokoro on 1st April 1873, the exact day upon which his term of service was to expire with the Khedive. To his great regret he learned, after his arrival, that Mr. Higginbotham, chief engineer of the expedition, had died at the end of February. The station had been much neglected since his departure; the environs were a mass of filth, and bones and old clothes lay scattered in every direction. Raouf Bey and the troops, however, appeared to be in good health. In his absence, a beautiful new screw-steamer had been built, the work of the Englishmen left at the station. She had been well constructed, and being without paddles, would be able to glide easily through the narrow channels of the Bahr Giraffe. The reinforcements received from Khartoum turned out to be merely slaves who had been sold to the Government and rapidly trained for soldiers.

Preparations were now made for the return homewards, and everything was ready by the 25th May. Parting with the 'Forty Thieves' after so many experiences together was rather a sad business; and as Baker walked down the line of troops, they broke the bounds of discipline by exclaiming: 'May God give you a long life! and may you meet your family in good health at home!' In the homeward journey, the passage through the Bahr Giraffe was found to be freer than on the upward journey. Three slave vessels belonging to Abou Saood were captured, and six hundred slaves were liberated. Arriving at Berber, Baker found a considerable improvement in the country; the Arabs had begun to return to the banks of the river, and to attend to agricultural matters. From Berber they marched to Souakim, on the Red Sea, going by steamer to Suez. Cairo was reached on 24th August, when Baker presented himself to his Highness the Khedive, and explained the large chart of new territory which had been annexed in Central Africa. Baker was honoured by receiving from the Khedive the Imperial Order of the Osmanie, second class, as a token of approval. The botanical collection prepared by Lady Baker throughout the journey was also handed to his Highness. These, along with samples of fibres, skins, and the salt of the new territory, were afterwards sent to the Vienna Exhibition.

Abou Saood, having been previously arrested by Baker's orders, was tried by a special tribunal, but afterwards released; and, much to Baker's astonishment, the news reached him when in England that he afterwards received a post under the Government.

The soldiers who had fought the battle of Masindi were suitably rewarded, and those who had particularly distinguished themselves were promoted. Before starting for England, a gratuity of a month's pay was given to every English engineer and mechanic. Baker, at the close of his journey, expressed his great thankfulness at the able assistance he, along with every member of the inland expedition, had received from his wife; also, that during a period of fourteen months he had lost but one man from sickness, out of a detachment of 212 officers and men.

His conclusions in Ismailia regarding the slave trade are, that a sweeping reform is necessary before commerce and civilisation can do their perfect work. Baker's suggestion on this point was to the effect 'that all the present existing traders or tenants of the White Nile should be expelled from the country, precisely as I had expelled them from the territory under my command.' 'The Government,' he remarks, 'might then assume the monopoly of the ivory trade of the White Nile; and the natives would in a few years be restored to confidence.' Adopting the words used in his *Albert Nyanza,* he further remarks: 'Should the slave trade be suppressed, there will be a good opening for the ivory trade. The conflicting trading parties being withdrawn, and the interest of the trade exhibited by a single company, the natives would no longer be able to barter ivory for cattle; thus they would be forced to accept other goods in exchange. The newly-discovered Albert lake opens the centre of Africa to navigation. Steamers ascend from Khartoum to Gondokoro, in lat. 4° 55'. Seven days' march south of that station the navigable portion of the Nile is reached, whence vessels can ascend direct to the Albert lake. Thus an enormous extent of country is opened to navigation; and Manchester goods and various other articles would find a ready market in exchange for ivory at a prodigious profit, as in those newly-discovered regions ivory has a merely nominal value.   Beyond this commencement of honest trade, I cannot offer a suggestion, as no produce of the country except ivory could afford the expense of transport to Europe. If Africa is to be civilised, it must be effected by commerce, which, once established, will open the way for missionary labour; but all ideas of commerce, improvement, and the advancement of the African race that philanthropy can suggest, must be discarded until the traffic in slaves shall have ceased to exist.   Should the slave trade be suppressed, a field would be opened the extent of which I will not attempt to suggest, as the future would depend upon the good government of countries now devoted to savage anarchy and confusion.   Difficult and almost impossible is the task before the missionary. The Austrian Mission has failed, and their stations have been forsaken; their pious labour was hopeless, and the devoted priests died upon their barren field.'

Baker remarks 'that those missionaries who may settle amongst the Baris must possess an inexhaustible stock of patience.'   The Madi and Shooli tribes he considers more capable of religious instruction.   From experience, he found that a good shot and a good sportsman always commanded the admiration of the natives.   Musical instruments, especially the bagpipes, would attract them greatly.   Conjuring tricks, the magic lantern, magnetic battery, dissolving views, photographic apparatus, and coloured pictorial illustrations, would all delight and amuse them greatly.   A good surgeon would always make his way; and devotional exercises should be chiefly musical. A liberal supply of such articles as beads, copper rods, brass rings for arms, fingers, and ears, gaudy cotton handkerchiefs, red or blue blankets, zinc mirrors, red cotton shirts, etc., distributed amongst them, would add greatly to his weight and influence. A knowledge of agriculture, with a stock of implements suited to the country, carpenters' and joiners' tools, are also necessary to the well-equipped missionary.

Baker's concluding remarks are in every respect admirable, and contain a summary of the work done by his expedition :—
'A paternal Government extended its protection through lands hitherto a field for anarchy and slavery. The territory within my rule was purged from the slave trade. The natives of the great Shooli tribe, relieved from their oppressors, clung to the protecting Government. The White Nile, for a distance of 1600 miles from Khartoum to Central Africa, was cleansed from the abomination of a traffic which had hitherto sullied its waters. Every cloud had passed away, and the term of my office expired in peace and sunshine. In this result I humbly traced God's blessing.'

Writing on 7th June 1879, a correspondent of the *Times* remarks regarding the work of Colonel Gordon, Baker's successor on the Nile, that his expeditions are a proof that Egypt has pushed herself farther into the country than her power of orderly rule can warrant. Brigands had harassed his path throughout the country, which had relapsed from a state of cultivation into a barren desert. Colonel Gordon made many salutary changes in the government, and sent back many useless Egyptians to Khartoum. His lieutenant, Gessi, had completely conquered the slave dealers of the Bahr Gazelle district.

HENRY M. STANLEY.

THIS is an age of newspapers: the daily sheet of news has so grown in importance as to be indispensable; it has also grown in power and influence. However little reading the business man or the average man of the world may go through, he must see the newspaper. They wield an ever-increasing influence in the growth of public opinion; if their leaders are not infallible, or the opinions they contain widely adopted, still they give an opportunity to the general public of forming opinions, and of gaining information regarding all matters of current and general interest. Time was when writing for the periodical press was an insignificant and ill-paid employment; now its contributors may be found amongst the rank and talent of the time; while for the regular staff, journalism is in every sense a highly respectable profession. To journalism, and to a daring journalist, we are indebted for two of the most important geographical feats of the time—the finding of Dr. Livingstone, and the crossing of the continent of Africa by way of the Congo. In the accomplishment of these two ends, Mr. H. M. Stanley must take a foremost place as a journalist and explorer.

Henry Moreland Stanley, one of the bravest and most daring journalists of the time, was born in Denbigh, North Wales, and while still in his teens, he emigrated to New Orleans. Joining the Confederate army, he was taken prisoner at the battle of Pittsburg Landing, on the 6th of April 1862. He effected his escape while being conveyed to prison, in a daring manner, and returned to England for a few months. Coming back to the United States, he enlisted in the Federal navy, and was present at the capture of Fort Fisher on the 15th January 1865. He acted as special correspondent for the *New York Tribune* after the war. In this capacity he accompanied General Hancock's expedition against the Kiowa and Cheyenne Indians. On his return, along with a companion of kindred spirit, he accomplished nearly seven hundred miles of the journey on a raft down the river Platte as far as its junction with the Missouri. At a later date, Stanley and two companions appeared at the American Consulate, Constantinople, in a totally destitute condition, having been robbed and maltreated in attempting to reach the interior of Asia Minor. Reaching New York, he was engaged on the staff of the *New York Herald* as special correspondent with the British military expedition to Magdala in Abyssinia. Before proceeding on his Livingstone search expedition, he had accomplished a journey from Constantinople, through Asia Minor, Persia, and India, to Bombay, with only a single servant as companion.

When Mr. H. M. Stanley, on returning to England in April 1874 from the Ashantee war, heard the news of the death of Dr. Livingstone, it awakened the determination within him, that, if his life was spared, he would proceed to Africa and finish his unaccomplished work. On finishing a new book on *Coomassie and Magdala* (where he had been as special war correspondent), his attention was directed to works upon Africa, its geography, geology, botany, and ethnology. Having already been four times on the African continent, the subjects had a living interest for him. His library of books on the subject consisted of over one hundred and thirty volumes. From these books and from his own personal experience he gained a knowledge of what had been already accomplished in discovery and exploration; and so he mapped out fresh ground, and made a list of instruments and other paraphernalia which would be found useful should a fresh journey be undertaken.

While in the office of the *Daily Telegraph* newspaper in London, and while the subject of journalistic enterprise in general was under discussion, the editor of the *Telegraph* asked Mr. Stanley a question about South African exploration.

'Could you, and would you, complete the work? And what is there to do?'

Stanley replied that 'the outlet of Lake Tanganyika is undiscovered. We know nothing scarcely, except what Speke has sketched out, of Lake Victoria; we do not even know whether it consists of one or many lakes, and therefore the sources of the Nile are still unknown. Moreover, the western half of the African continent is still a white blank.'

'Do you think you can settle all this, if we commission you?'

'While I live, there will be something done. If I survive the time required to perform all the work, all shall be done.'

Mr. James Gordon Bennett of the *New York Herald*, who had a prior claim to Mr. Stanley's services, was communicated with by telegraph, and asked if he would join the *Telegraph* newspaper in sending Stanley out to Africa to complete the discoveries of Speke, Burton, and Livingstone. The answer received was, ' Yes. Bennett.'

Nothing now remained but to complete his preparations as swiftly as possible. Two weeks were allowed for purchasing boats,—a yawl, a gig, and a barge,—and for giving orders for the other articles of his equipment. The barge he had constructed on a special plan of his own ; it was to be forty feet long, six feet beam, and thirty inches deep, of Spanish cedar three-eighths of an inch thick. Three men were engaged to go with him, two of them being Francis John Pocock and Edward Pocock, sons of a fisherman 'of Lower Upnor, Kent, and Frederick Barker, a clerk at the Langham Hotel in London. Numberless other requests from parties who wished to join the expedition were refused. A journey was also undertaken to America to take farewell of friends.

Before leaving, Mr. Stanley received many tokens of regard from numerous friends. Two farewell dinners were also accepted, one given by the editor of the *Daily Telegraph*, the other by the representative of the *New York Herald*. Mr. Stanley, with his three Europeans, and all the general property of the expedition, left for Zanzibar on the 15th August 1874. They arrived there on the 21st September. The following gives the feeling of the traveller on sighting the island : ' As he passes close to the deeply-verdant shores of Zanzibar island, he views nature robed in the greenest verdure, with a delightful freshness of leaf, exhaling fragrance to the incoming wanderer. He is wearied with the natural deep blue of the ocean, and eager for any change. He remembers the unconquerable aridity and the dry, bleached heights he last saw, and, lo ! what a change ! Responding to his half-formed wish, the earth rises before him verdant,

prolific, bursting with fatness.   Palms raise their feathery
heads and mangoes their great globes of dark-green foliage;
banana plantations with impenetrable shade, groves of orange,
fragrant cinnamon, and spreading bushy clove, diversify and
enrich the landscape.   Jack-fruit trees loom up with great
massive crowns of leaf and branch, while between the trees
and in every open space succulent grapes and plants cover
the soil with a thick garment of verdure.   There is nothing
grand or sublime in the view before him, and his gaze is
not attracted to any special feature, because all is toned down
to a uniform softness by the exhalation rising from the warm
heaving bosom of the island.'   Arrived at Zanzibar, the preparations for the journey were commenced.   All the varied
articles which would be of use in dealing with the natives
were bought and selected.   There were different kinds of
cloth, beads, and wire, bales of unbleached cotton, striped
and coloured fabrics, handkerchiefs and red caps, bags of
blue, green, red, white, and amber-coloured beads, small and
large, round and oval, and coils of thick brass wire.

The character of the Sultan of Zanzibar, Barghash bin Sayid,
is drawn in an amiable light by Mr. Stanley.   An Arab prince,
educated in the school of Islam, at the request of the
Government of Britain he became an opponent of the slave
trade.   The first decided steps taken by the British Government were due to the letters written by Dr. Livingstone on
the subject.   The territories over which he is an independent
prince are the islands of Zanzibar, Pemba, and Mafia, about
a thousand miles of coast; Mr. Stanley calculates that his
power extends over an area of 20,000 square miles, with a
population of half a million.   The following articles of commerce are exported :—Cloves, cinnamon, tortoise-shell, pepper,

copal gum, ivory, orchilla weed, india-rubber, and hides.
Caoutchouc is abundant, but not yet utilized; the cocoa-nut
palm flourishes, also the sugar-cane; rice is grown on the
banks of the Rufiji; cotton would also thrive if cultivated.
In order to utilize the products of East Africa, a tramway
into the interior is required, as cutting roads through jungles
and using waggons are only temporary conveniences. The
Arabs of Zanzibar are described as the best of their race,
being sociable, frank, good-natured, and hospitable, staunch
friends and desperate haters. The Arab gentleman has very
perfect manners, and never broaches delicate matters before
strangers.

Mr. Stanley engaged at once all those who had been
employed in the Livingstone Search Expedition of 1872, as
servants in the present expedition. Numberless applications
were made for employment by the most unlikely subjects:
cripples, the palsied, the consumptive, and the superannuated
were amongst the number, and so a selection had to be made.
Many were engaged, however, whose characters would not
bear inspection. The customary presents were bestowed on
these servants, and a preliminary palaver was engaged in,
when the difficulties of the journey were duly discussed.
When the *Lady Alice* arrived in four sections, Mr. Stanley
gave orders that she should be reduced in weight by some
slight remodelling. A devout Moslem, Turya Topau by name,
supplied the explorer with cloth, cottons, and kanikis at
reasonable prices, and accepted his bills on Mr. Joseph M.
Levy of the *Daily Telegraph*. When all his stores were
collected, consisting of cloth, beads, wire, medicine, clothes,
tents, ammunition, provisions, instruments, stationery, and
photographic apparatus, etc., they weighed in all over eight

tons. These articles, when divided into loads of sixty pounds, required the capacity of three hundred men to carry them. A payment in money of four months' wages in advance was made to these men. The entire amount disbursed in pay and rations amounted to nearly £1300.

Leaving Zanzibar, they sailed for Bagamoyo, on the mainland, which they reached on 13th November. Some disturbances occurred in the town on the arrival of such a motley crowd of followers ; but these, however, were quelled.

In speaking of the small results which have attended missionary labour on the east coast of Africa, Mr. Stanley ventures to give his own opinions on the subject. These opinions are worthy of careful remark, coming as they do from such an indefatigable explorer. 'It is strange,' he writes, 'how British philanthropists, clerical and lay, persist in the delusion that the Africans can be satisfied with spiritual improvement only. They should endeavour to impress themselves with the undeniable fact, that man, white, yellow, red, or black, has also material wants which crave to be understood and supplied. A barbarous man is a pure materialist. He is full of cravings for possessing something that he cannot describe. He is like a child which has not yet acquired the faculty of articulation. The missionary discovers the barbarian almost stupefied with brutish ignorance, with the instincts of a man in him, but yet living the life of a beast. Instead of attempting to develop the qualities of this practical human being, he instantly attempts his transformation, by expounding to him the dogmas of the Christian faith, the doctrine of transubstantiation, and other difficult subjects, before the barbarian has had time to articulate his necessities, and to explain to him that he is a frail creature, requiring to be fed with

bread, and not with a stone. My experience and study of
the pagan prove to me, however, that if the missionary can
show the poor materialist that religion is allied with substantial benefits and improvement of his degraded condition,
the task to which he is about to devote himself will be rendered comparatively easy. For the African, once brought
in contact with the European, becomes docile enough : he is
awed by a consciousness of his own immense inferiority, and
imbued with a vague hope that he may also rise in time to
the level of this superior being, who has so challenged his
admiration. It is the story of Caliban and Stefano over again.
He comes to him with a desire to be taught, and, seized with
an ambition to aspire to a higher life, becomes docile and
tractable ; but, to his surprise, he perceives himself mocked by
this being, who talks to him about matters that he despairs of
ever understanding, and therefore, with abashed face and a still
deeper sense of his inferiority, he retires to his den, cavern,
or hut, with a dogged determination to be contented with the
brutish life he was born in.'

The start for the interior was made on the morning of the
17th November 1874, when the quantity and quality of the
loads were distributed according to the strength and disposi-
tion of the carriers. The following was the order in which the
expedition filed out of Bagamoyo :—' Four chiefs, a few
hundred yards in front; next the twelve guides, clad in red
robes of Jobo, bearing the wire coils; then a long file,
270 strong, bearing cloth, wire, beads, and sections of the
Lady Alice ; after them, thirty-six women and ten boys,
children of some of the chiefs and boat-bearers, following their
mothers and assisting them with trifling loads of utensils,
followed by the riding asses, Europeans, and gun-bearers;

the long line closed by sixteen chiefs who act as rear-guard, and whose duties are to pick up stragglers, and act as supernumeraries until other men can be procured : in all, three hundred and fifty-six souls connected with the Anglo-American Expedition. The lengthy line occupies nearly half a mile of the path which, at the present day, is the commercial and exploring highway into the lake regions.' Edward Pocock acted as bugler. Hamadi, the chief guide, was also supplied with a prodigiously long ivory horn, which was used when approaching a suitable camping-place. A boy walked before Hamadi with a native drum, which he was to beat only when in the neighbourhood of villages. The momentous journey had begun in a most auspicious manner.

The first halt was made at Kikoka on the 18th of November. After leaving Kikoka and Rosako, and passing through a stretch of beautiful park land, 'green as an English lawn, dipping into lovely vales, and rising into gentle ridges,' the small village of Pongwe was reached on the 23d. The populous village of Congorido was reached on the 24th. Mfutch was the next village, in the neighbourhood of which flourished the baobab, the doum, borassus, and the fan palm. Game was numerous on the march between Mfutch and Rubuti. They had crossed the river Wami three times that day. The Mkundi river was reached on the 3d December. Simba-Mwenni, the Lion Lord, owning five villages in this neighbourhood, presented Mr. Stanley with a sheep, some flour, and plantains. In return, he was presented with some cloth. In this march to Makubika, the next settlement, they attained an altitude of 2675 feet above the level of the sea, and were surrounded with grand and impressive scenery. Between Mamboya and Kitangeh, he was struck with the resemblance which many of the scenes bore to others which he had seen in the Alleghanies. Water was abundant, and, when nearing Kitangeh, villages were found dotting every hill. By way of providing food for the camp, Mr. Stanley shot two zebras near Kitangeh. Crossing a plain, six miles in width, Tubugwe was reached. In passing, fourteen human skulls were noted, evidently the relics of unfortunate travellers slain by an attack of the Wahumba from the north-west. After twenty-five days' march from Bagamoyo, Mpwapwa was reached on the 12th December.

Mpwapwa is a collection of villages situated on a stream of the same name, at the base of the southern slope of a range of mountains extending from Chunyu to Ugombo. Desertions were now becoming frequent; fifty men had abandoned the expedition before reaching Mpwapwa. By a route skirting the Marenga Mkali desert, they reached Chunyu, an exposed place which overlooked the desert separating Usagara from Ugogo. On the 10th December, Ugogo was entered. The principal features of the landscape were now a broad black plain, on which were spread out a few solitary baobab trees, some wattled enclosures inhabited by the natives, and occasional herds of cattle or flocks of goats. Halting at Zingeh on Christmas day 1874, the encampment presented a very forlorn appearance. Food was becoming scarce. The leader of the expedition was reduced to live upon boiled rice, tea, and coffee. The natives were miserable and dispirited beneath the deluge of rain, which lasted several days. The Mukondoku district, which was reached on the 29th December, contained about a hundred small villages. The natives made a warlike show at first, but calmed down into a more pacific demeanour. The king, by name Calula, was noted as being crafty and unscrupulous, and extortionate in his tribute upon travellers. Receiving guides from the king, on the 1st January 1875 they struck north, leaving for the first time the path to Unyanyembe.   On the way, young Keelusu, the son of a chief, presented the leader of the expedition with a gallon of new milk.   After this present had been substantially acknowledged, he divined with his sandals, and predicted that the journey would be successful.   Halting at Mtiwi on 2d January 1875, the aneroid showed that they had reached an altitude of 2825 feet.   The night spent here was a disturbed one, as the camp was flooded with water, owing to a rainfall of six inches of water.   Ugogo was left behind, and the district of Uyanzi was reached on 4th January.   The plains of Ugogo furnished only dwarf bushes of acacia, rank-smelling gum-trees, and euphorbias, but the character of the vegetation was now much improved.   The village of Kashongwa, situated on the verge of a trackless wild, was reached on 6th January.   The way to the next halting-place, called Urimi, was covered with a vast carpet of scrub or brush, through which the expedition could only make its way with extreme difficulty.   Reaching the neighbourhood of a miserable village called Uveriveri, food was not to be obtained, and they were on the verge of starvation.   The pangs of hunger were relieved by a mixture of boiled oatmeal and 'revalenta Arabica.'   Reaching Suna on 12th January, they found the natives not altogether friendly. The Warimi tribe possessed a fine physique, being robust, tall, and manly in bearing.   The ornaments they wore were cinctures of brass wire round the loins, armlets and leglets of brass, brass-wire collars, and beads plentifully besprinkled amongst their hair.   In consequence of the privations undergone in Ugogo, many of the men were now on the sick list, and

Edward Pocock was attacked with fever. Pushing on, weary and harassed, Chiwyu was reached, where Pocock died on 17th January. He was buried in English fashion beneath the shade of a large acacia tree, the prayers of the Church Service were read over his remains, and his brother carved a cross on the trunk of the tree as an emblem of the faith in which he died.

The height at which the expedition had camped at Chiwyu was 5400 feet above sea level. 'To the northward of Suna and Chiwyu,' writes Mr. Stanley, 'the country, however, no longer retained that grand unfurrowed uplift, but presented several isolated hills and short ranges, while to the westward also we saw that it was divided into oval basins, rimmed with low hills. From these same hollows and furrows and basins at the base of the hills, scattered to the north and west of Suna and Chiwyu, issue the first tiny rivulets which, as we continue our journey to the north-west, gradually converge to one main stream, trending towards Lake Victoria. It is in this region, therefore, that the most extreme southern sources of the Nile were discovered.' The springs and headquarters of the Shimuyu, flowing north-north-west into Lake Victoria, were here crossed several times. After passing Mangura, the district of Ituru was entered. The streams here, being numerous, flowed northwards. In spite of the amount of water, however, the cattle were poor and gaunt, the dogs half-starved, and the sheep and goats perfect skeletons. Amongst the birds seen in this region were spur-winged geese, brown short-billed ducks, long-legged plovers, snipes, cranes, herons, spoonbills, paroquets, and jays. The wealth of the villagers in Ituru consisted in their cattle and asses. A village called Vinyata was reached on 21st January. Sickness was increasing in the camp;

twenty men had already died, and eighty-nine had deserted since leaving the coast. Two men belonging to the expedition were brutally murdered in this neighbourhood; and although the magic doctor who visited the camp was handsomely treated, the natives showed such an amount of treachery and hostility as made self-defence imperative. In the second day's encounter twenty-one soldiers and one messenger were killed, and three wounded. Another encounter, with the view of driving back the natives to a greater distance, took place on the 25th. On summing up the disasters at the close of this day, it was found that in all twenty-four men had been killed and four wounded; besides this, there were twenty-five on the sick list. This number of men rendered useless caused a re-arrangement of the burdens and baggage of the camp; and much of the miscellaneous property was burned ere the 26th, after which the journey was resumed. The expedition at this time consisted of three Europeans, two hundred and six Wangwana and Wanyamwezi, twenty-five women, and six boys. Ten miles from Vinyata another halt was made, at an altitude of 5650 feet above the ocean. They had on one side of them 'the deep, wooded valley through which the rapid Leewumbu rushes. Its banks on each side slope steeply upward, and at the top become detached hills clothed with forest; from their base wave the uplands in grand and imposing wooded ridges.'

Reaching Mgongo Tembo, Mr. Stanley made friends with the chief of the same name, from whom he heard that Mirambo was fighting the Wasukuma farther forward. After a halt of two days, they pushed forward, entering Mangura in Usukuma. Six miles west was Igira, overlooking the plain of Luwamberri. This plain, nearly forty miles broad, stretched N.N.W. towards the Victoria lake; from its low altitude and the wave-worn appearance of the higher elevations, Mr. Stanley concluded that it must have been at one time a long arm of the great lake. A plentiful supply of meat for the camp was secured in crossing. Mr. Stanley shot one day a giraffe and a small antelope; next day, five zebra; the third day, on the western verge, he shot two gnu, one buffalo, and a zebra, besides two spur-winged geese, four guinea - fowl, and five ducks.

When Mombiti in the Usukuma country was reached, provisions were plentiful, and the whole expedition revelled in abundance. Moving northwards, Usiha was reached on the 17th February. 'Usiha,' says Mr. Stanley, 'is the commencement of a most beautiful pastoral country, which terminates only in the Victoria Nyanza. From the summit of one of the weird grey rock piles which characterize it, one may enjoy the unspeakable fascination of an apparently boundless horizon. On all sides there stretches toward it the face of a vast circle replete with peculiar features, of detached hills, great crag masses of riven and sharply-angled rock, and outcropping mounds, between which heaves and rolls in low, broad waves a green, grassy plain, whereon feed thousands of cattle scattered about in small herds.' Mr. Stanley revelled for a while in this prospect, and felt 'as gratified as though I possessed the wand of an enchanter, and had raised around me the verdant downs of Sussex.' When the expedition started again over these fair plains on the 19th, they moved with a greater sense of freedom than they had hitherto enjoyed in marching up from the coast. To Abaddi, which was reached on 21st February, the country was clear and open, with scarce a tree or shrub; the grass was only an inch high. The native men stalked about stark naked, but the women were clad with stiff skins and half-tanned cow hides. The plains were whitened with herds of cattle, and flocks of goats and sheep. Marya was the next camp; here the natives were impertinent. Kagehyi, on Lake Victoria Nyanza, was reached on 27th February. On summing up the number of miles gone over since leaving the coast, he found them to be seven hundred and twenty.

Fairly settled at Kagehyi, on Speke Gulf, arrangements were made for sailing round Lake Victoria Nyanza. The news spread that the white man had arrived, and traders flocked in to sell their commodities, consisting of dried fish, cassava, ripe bananas, potatoes, and yams. Prince Kaduma, with whom Stanley had several interviews, was a victim of pombé, the native beer, made from fermented grain or coarse flour. This he drank in large quantities several times a day, generally reeling to his cot in a state of intoxication every night. At first Mr. Stanley had hopes that Kaduma would accompany him round the lake, but he was disappointed. While the *Lady Alice* was being prepared for the journey, the natives treated the Wangwana to most extraordinary accounts of people dwelling on its shores who were gifted with tails, of others who trained enormous and fierce dogs for war, and a tribe of cannibals preferring human flesh to all other kinds of food. When the boat was provided with the necessary stores for the voyage, ten sailors and a steersman were selected. Fred Barker and Frank Pocock were left in charge of the camp, and on 8th March 1875 they set sail on that part of the lake since known, in honour of its discoverer, as Speke Gulf.

In coasting round the lake a variety of fortunes attended them. At Ugamba they were troubled with the natives, many of whom were intoxicated, and who insisted that they should visit their King Kamoydah. Escaping from them, the natives of Namungi showed a most ardent desire to do business, selling them provisions sufficient for three days, consisting of bananas, fowls and eggs, and sweet maramba or native wine. About thirty of their canoes, the crews of which were all intoxicated, followed them for a few miles. Near Mombiti they were mobbed by the natives with intent to steal. In the bay of Buka, at the north end of the lake, the Mtongoleh invited them to his village, feasting them with clotted milk, mellow and ripe bananas, a kid, sweet potatoes, and eggs, and also despatched a messenger to Mtesa, king of Uganda, announcing the coming of a stranger. The bay of Buka was picturesque, the margin being lined by waving water-cane, and up to the highest hill-top all was verdure of varying shades. Leaving this delightful spot, they halted at Kirudo, where they were met by six beautiful canoes containing a deputation from Mtesa. The commander, a fine lusty young man of about twenty, springing into their boat, knelt down and delivered his errand in the following words :—

'The kabaka sends me with many salaams to you. He is in great hopes that you will visit him, and has encamped at Usavara, that he may be near the lake when you come. He does not know from what land you have come, but I have a swift messenger with a canoe who will not stop until he gives all the news to the *kabaka.* His mother dreamed a dream a few nights ago, and in her dream she saw a white man on this lake in a boat coming this way, and the next morning she told the *kabaka*, and, lo! you have come. Give me your answer, that I may send the messenger. Ywizanzi—yanzi—yanzi !' (Thanks, thanks, thanks.)

Rowing to the village of Kadzi, the young commander, after receiving all the news, determined to show his power, and ordered the sub-chief of the village to bring forth the best they had wherewith to treat the stranger. Two bullocks and four goats, a basketful of fat mellow bananas, and four two-gallon jars of maramba were brought, and ample justice was done to them. Magassa helped himself to three bullocks, cut down as many bananas as they wished, and also made free amongst the chickens. Mr. Stanley at first concluded that this must be a wonderful land, when the mere mention of the *kabaka's* name had such an effect. Arrived at Usavara, the *kabaka's* hunting village, they received an ostentatious welcome from King Mtesa. Mr. Stanley was strongly impressed with his power and intelligence. 'Mtesa,' he writes, 'has impressed me as being an intelligent and distinguished prince, who, if aided in time by virtuous philanthropists, will do more for Central Africa than fifty years of gospel teaching, unaided by such authority, can do. I think I see in him the light that shall lighten the darkness of this benighted region; a prince well worthy of the most hearty sympathies that Europe can give him. . . . I saw over 3000 soldiers of Mtesa nearly half civilised. I saw about a hundred chiefs who might be classed in the same scale as the men of Zanzibar and Oman, clad in as rich robes, and armed in the same fashion, and have witnessed with astonishment such order and law as is obtainable in semi-civilised countries. All this is the result of a poor Moslem's labour; his name is Muley bin Salim. He it was who first began teaching here the doctrines of Islam.'

The personal appearance of this powerful emperor he has thus sketched:—'In person Mtesa is tall, probably 6 feet 1 inch, and slender. He has very intelligent and agreeable features, reminding me of some of the faces of the great stone images at Thebes, and of the statues in the museum at Cairo. He has the same fulness of lips, but their grossness is relieved by the general expression of amiability blended with dignity that pervades his face; and the large, lustrous, lambent eyes that lend it a strange beauty, and are typical of the race from which I believe him to be sprung.'

It seemed to Stanley, when he saw the brown skins of the natives, their brown robes and canoes, that brown must be the national colour. A young crocodile had been found some little distance away. 'Now, Stamlee,' said Mtesa, 'show my women how white men can shoot.' The explorer was fortunate enough to shoot the crocodile, nearly severing its head from its body at a distance of 100 yards. From the hunting lodges of Usavara, Stanley followed Mtesa to his capital, a cluster of huts situated on a hill-top, called Rabaga. The palace was a spacious, lofty, barn-like structure. The view from the hill-top was charming. 'On all sides rolled in grand waves a voluptuous land of sunshine, and plenty, and early summer verdure, cooled by soft breezes from the great equatorial fresh-water sea. Isolated hill-cones, similar to that of Rabaga, or square tabular masses, rose up from the beautiful landscape to attract, like mysteries, the curious stranger's observation; and villages and banana groves of still fresher green, far removed on the crest of distant swelling ridges, announced that Mtesa owned a land worth loving. Dark sinuous lines traced the winding courses of deep ravines filled with trees, and grassy extents of gently undulating ground marked the pastures; broader depressions suggested the cultivated gardens and the grain fields; while, on the far verge of the horizon, we saw the beauty and the charm of the land melting into the blue of distance.' Round the imperial palace, which was spacious and lofty, were clean courtyards, with quarters for the harem and the guards, with a cane enclosure surrounding all. In the course of his interviews with Mtesa, Mr. Stanley explained to the great African potentate the leading doctrines of the Christian religion, leaving it with himself and his chiefs to decide as to whether Christ or Mohammed was the worthier character. He also sketched a history of religious beliefs from Adam to Mohammed, and commenced the translation of the Ten Commandments. While this lasted, Mtesa and his principal chiefs were so absorbed that little business was done.

During Stanley's residence, the court of Mtesa was visited by another white man, M. Linant de Bellefonds, a member of the Gordon-Pasha Expedition. The two men passed many pleasant hours together, joining in the religious conversations with Mtesa, and agreeing so closely in what was said as to astonish him. Stanley parted with Linant on the morning of 17th April 1875, starting for Kagehyi with the promise that he would return again within a month. Unforeseen circumstances prevented his return at so early a date. He afterwards found that Colonel Linant had remained six weeks waiting for him. In afterwards journeying northwards, he was killed by the natives.

Mr. Stanley, in letters written to the *Daily Telegraph* and the *New York Herald* from Usavara, made a strong appeal for a Christian mission to be sent to King Mtesa. 'It is not,' he wrote, 'the mere preacher, however, that is wanted here. The bishops of Great Britain collected, with all the classic youth of Oxford and Cambridge, would effect nothing by mere talk with the intelligent people of Uganda. It is the practical

Christian tutor, who can teach people how to become Christians, cure their diseases, construct dwellings, understand and exemplify agriculture, and turn his hand to anything, like a sailor,—this is the man who is wanted. Such an one, if he can be found, would become the saviour of Africa. He must be tied to no church or sect, but profess God and His Son and the moral law; and live a blameless Christian life, inspired by liberal principles, charity to all men, and devout faith in Heaven.'

In the return journey to Kagehyi, a halt was made at Makongo, on the coast of Uzongora. They found that the place nestled in a sheltered nook, in a bay-like indentation of the lofty mountain wall, and was crowded with banana groves and huts. The natives appeared friendly at first; but before Stanley left, they tried to pick a quarrel with him regarding the drawing up of their canoes on the beach, and they made a show of fighting. A better understanding prevailed before leaving; and the chief of Makongo presented them with ten bunches of green bananas, or sufficient for one day's provisions. Visiting Musira Island, about three miles from Makongo, Mr. Stanley, with all the ardour of a boy, enjoyed a solitary exploration of the place. The island he found to be about three-quarters of a mile long and about two hundred yards wide. Expatiating on the prospect, he wrote:—' It is a spot from which, undisturbed, the eye may rove over one of the strangest yet fairest portions of Africa—hundreds of square miles of beautiful lake scenes; a great length of grey plateau wall, upright and steep, but indented with exquisite inlets, half surrounded with embowering plantains; hundreds of square miles of pastoral upland, dotted thickly with villages and groves of banana. From my lofty eyrie I can see herds

upon herds of cattle, and many minute specks, white and
black, which can be nothing but flocks of sheep and goats.
I can also see pale-blue columns of ascending smoke from the
fires, and upright thin figures moving about. Secure on my
lofty throne, I can view their movements, and laugh at the
ferocity of the savage hearts which beat in those dark figures;
for I am a part of nature now, and for the present as invulner-
able as itself. As little do they know that human eyes survey
their forms from the summit of this lake-girt isle, as that the
eyes of the Supreme in heaven are upon them. How long, I
wonder, shall the people of these lands remain thus ignorant
of Him who created the gorgeous sunlit world they look upon
each day from their lofty upland? How long shall their
untamed ferocity be a barrier to the Gospel; and how long
shall they remain unvisited by the Teacher? What a land
they possess, and what an inland sea! How steamers afloat
on the lake might cause Ururi to shake hands with Uzongora,
and Uganda with Usukuma; make the wild Wavuma friends
with the Waziuza, and unite the Wakerewe with the Wagana.
A great trading port might then spring up on the Shimeyu,
whence the coffee of Uzongora; the ivory, sheep, and goats of
Ugeyeya, Usoga, Uvuma, and Uganda; the cattle of Uwya,
Karagwe, Usagara, Ihangiro, and Usukuma; the myrrh, cassia,
and furs and hides of Uganda and Uddu; the rice of
Ukerewe; and the grain of Uziuza, might be exchanged for
the fabrics brought from the coast,—all the land be redeemed
from wilderness, the industry and energy of the natives stimulated, the havoc of the slave trade stopped, and all the
countries round about permeated with the nobler ethics of a
higher humanity. But at present the hands of the people are
lifted—murder in their hearts—one against the other; ferocity

is kindled at sight of the wayfarer; the people of Ugeyeya and Wasoga go stark naked; Mtesa impales, burns, and maims his victims; the Wirigedi lie in wait along their shores for the stranger, and the slingers of the islands practise their art against him; the Wakara poison anew their deadly arrows at sight of a canoe; and each tribe, with rage and hate in its heart, remains aloof from the other. " Verily, the dark places of the earth are full of the habitations of cruelty." '

They next touched at Alice island, which they found clothed with abundance of coarse grass. ' The ravines and hollows are choked with a luxuriance of vegetable life,—trees, plants, ferns, ground orchids, and wild pine-apples.' The natives here asked such an exorbitant price for what they had to sell, that they were unable to secure more than a few ears of corn. A miserable night was passed, after leaving Alice island, at Baker's island, the easternmost of the Bumbireh group. Bum-bireh is about eleven miles in length by two miles greatest breadth, containing about fifty small villages, with an average population of about 4000. Mr. Stanley and his company, with hunger gnawing at their vitals, were determined to risk something in order to secure a supply of food. In spite of the fact that the natives were rushing down the slopes and uttering fierce ejaculations, they pulled into a cove near the south-east end of Bumbireh. Stanley ordered the men to cease rowing; but they, saying that all the noise made by the natives was but savage bluster, pushed ashore. As the boat neared the water's edge, some of the men lifted great stones, and others prepared their bows; these they dropped after an exchange of greetings and pretended friendship. Suddenly the boat was seized and dragged about twenty yards high and dry over the rocky beach, much to the astonishment of those inside. ' Then ensued a

scene,' says Stanley, 'which beggars description. Pande-
monium—all its devils armed—raged around us. A forest of
spears was levelled; thirty or forty bows were drawn taut; as
many barbed arrows seemed already on the wing; thick,
knotty clubs waved over our heads; two hundred screaming
black demons jostled with each other and struggled for room
to vent their fury, or for an opportunity to deliver one crushing
blow or thrust at us.'

Their quiet demeanour had an effect. Mr. Stanley assumed
a resigned air, though he still retained his revolvers. Baraka
addressed them in these words: ' What, my friends, ails you?
Do you fear empty hands and smiling people like us? We are
friends; we came as friends to buy food, two or three bananas,
a few mouthfuls of grain, or potatoes, or cassava, and, if you
permit us, we shall depart as friends.' The oars were taken
away from the boat, and they were thus rendered helpless;
a council was held over them, when it was decided that they
were to remain there until the following day. Later in that
day, by a dexterous movement, Stanley managed to dodge the
natives and push the boat forward into the lake. The natives
were baffled and furious, and rushing down to the edge of
the lake, launched their canoes, and pursued them vigorously.
Several shots were fired, killing five or six of the natives,
when they attempted nothing further. On resuming their
paddles, they heard a voice cry out, 'Go and die in the
Nyanza,' and several arrows fell harmlessly near them.

Seventy-six hours after leaving Alice island they anchored
on an uninhabited island, where provisions were secured after
their long fast. The camp at Kagehyi was reached on 6th
May, much to the joy of the men there. To his sorrow,
however, Stanley found that Fred. Barker and two faithful

servants were dead. Affairs had gone well otherwise in the camp : the stores had been economically dealt out, and the Wangwana had recovered from the miserable attenuation caused by their march from the coast, and were now robust and fat. Stanley, after his return, was postrated by fever, which weakened him much, and reduced him about seven pounds in weight.

Making a bargain with Lukongeh, king of Ukerewe, for a certain number of canoes, Stanley prepared to embark on the return journey to Uganda as arranged. Many of these canoes were unseaworthy, and on the first night five of them were lost, with five guns, one case of ammunition, and twelve hundred pounds of grain. No lives were lost, owing to the energetic measures taken to reach the island of Miandereh. In order to punish the natives of Bumbireh for their former dastardly conduct, and for the killing of one of his men and the wounding of other eight, Stanley took the opportunity of inflicting a severe blow upon them, fighting with them from the lake until they were intimidated. Six of his men subsequently died from the effects of their wounds before reaching Uganda.

The result of Stanley's circumnavigation of the Victoria Nyanza was to prove that there is but one outlet from the lake, the Ripon Falls. There are three rivers, the Nagombwa, the Zedziwa, and the Mwerango, all of which flow into the lake. 'The Nagombwa empties into the Victoria Nile not far from Urondogani ; the Zedziwa empties into the Victoria Nile near Urondogani ; and Mwerango flows into the Mianja, the Mianja flows into the Kafu, and the Kafu into the Victoria Nile, somewhere in the neighbourhood of Rionga's island.'

Long before they arrived for the second time in Uganda,

greetings had been received from King Mtesa, proving the strength of his friendship. On their arrival, they found him at war with the rebellious people of Uvuma, who had been refusing to pay tribute, had harassed the coast of Chagwe, and stolen his people, 'selling them afterwards for a few bunches of bananas.' Mtesa also mentioned that it was not customary in Uganda to permit any stranger to leave until the war in which they were engaged was finished. When the war was finished, he would send a chief with an army to conduct him by the shortest route to the Nyanza (Muta N'zige). Mr. Stanley, assured that the war would not last long, resolved to stay and witness its progress, and in the meantime endeavour to gain information about the country and the people. In computing Mtesa's strength, he calculated that an army of 150,000 warriors had been gathered together. Including women and children, there could not be fewer than 250,000 souls in Mtesa's camp. Stanley was the witness of a fight in canoes. The Uganda war fleet numbered three hundred and twenty-five large and small canoes. The largest canoe was seventy-two feet in length, seven feet three inches in breadth, and four feet deep within. It could accommodate sixty-four paddlers besides the pilot. There were over a hundred canoes between fifty and seventy feet in length, and about fifty between thirty and fifty feet long; the other eighty canoes were of various sizes, from eighteen to thirty feet long. They would require a force of nearly 8600 men to man them.

In the intervals of warfare between the Waganda and the Wavuma, Stanley had several interesting conversations with Mtesa. A talk on the nature of angels led to a reference to the Bible, and from this reference sprang a desire on the part of Mtesa to possess a copy of the Holy Scriptures. A boy named Dallington, a pupil of the Universities Mission at Zanzibar, was started with the translation of a portion of the Bible into Kiswahili. With abundance of writing material at hand, the translation made rapid progress, and when completed, Mtesa was in possession of an abridged Protestant Bible in Kiswahili, containing all the principal events from the creation to the crucifixion of Christ. St. Luke's Gospel was given in a complete form. When this Bible was compiled, Mtesa called his chiefs together. After giving a history of his life in brief, relating his conversion from gross heathenism to Mohammedanism, he said : ' Now, God be thanked, a white man, "Stamlee," has come to Uganda with a book older than the Koran of Mohammed, and Stamlee says that Mohammed was a liar, and much of his book taken from this ; and this boy and Idi have read to me all that Stamlee has read to them from this book, and I find that it is a great deal better than the book of Mohammed, besides it is the first and oldest book. The prophet Moses wrote some of it a long, long time before Mohammed was even heard of, and the book was finished long before Mohammed was born. As Kintu, our first king, was a long time before me, so Moses was before Mohammed. Now I want you, my chiefs and soldiers, to tell me what we shall do. Shall we believe in Isa (Jesus) and Musa (Moses), or in Mohammed ? '

Chambarago replied : ' Let us take that which is the best.'

The Katekiro said : ' We know not which is the best. The Arabs say their book is the best, and white men say their book is the best ; how then can we know which speaks the truth ? '

After some further discussion, they all said, ' We will take the white man's book.' So Mtesa renounced his old religion of Islamism, and professed himself a convert, announcing his determination to adhere to his new religion, and build a church, and do all in his power to promote Christian sentiment amongst his people. Stanley offered to release Dallington from his service, in order that he might remain with Mtesa and read the Bible to him. On parting with him at this time, he said, ' Stamlee, say to the white people, when you write to them, that I am like a man sitting in darkness, or born blind, and that all I ask is that I may be taught how to see, and I shall continue a Christian while I live.' Stanley admitted, however, that his conversion was only nominal, and that a few months' talk about Christ and His work upon earth was not sufficient to eradicate the evils consequent upon thirty-five years' sensuous and brutal indulgence. The presence of a painstaking missionary would be required.

The war between Mtesa and the Wavuma was terminated on the 13th October 1875. Stanley helped this consummation not a little by inventing a floating fort, which moved towards the Wavuma, garrisoned with 214 men, but all of whom were hidden within. Steering directly towards the island of Ingira, where the enemy was stationed, a mysterious and stentorian voice was heard to shout from within, addressing the Wavuma : ' Speak. What will you do? Will you make peace and submit to Mtesa, or shall we blow up the island? Be quick and answer.'

This structure, totally unlike anything previously seen in these waters, appealed to their superstitious feelings, and the reply came from a chief: ' Enough ; let Mtesa be satisfied. We will collect the tribute to-day, and will come to Mtesa. Return, O spirit; the war is ended !' At these words the strange structure moved back to the cove where it had been constructed amidst the shouts of the assembled multitude. The tribute, consisting of several tusks of ivory and two young girls, was paid, and so the war ended.

The average Uganda peasant, according to Stanley, appears to be healthy and contented. The productions of the land are ivory, coffee, gums, resins, myrrh; lion, leopard, otter, and goat skins, ox-hides, snow-white monkey-skins, bark cloth, cattle, sheep, and goats. The principal vegetable productions are the papaw, banana, plantain, yams, sweet potatoes, peas, beans, melons, cucumbers, vegetable marrow, manioc, and tomatoes. The grains found in the neighbourhood of the capital are—wheat, rice, maize, sesamum, millet, and vetches. The soil of the lake coast region is described as of inexhaustible fertility. The banana plant is one of the most important and useful to the natives of Uganda. There are several varieties, and one which is unfit for food is used in the manufacture of wine. The fronds of the banana serve as thatch for houses, fences for enclosures, and as bedding. They are also used as table-cloths, wrappers, and pudding-cloths. The stems are used for fences and enclosures. The pith or heart of the stalk forms an excellent sponge. The fibres are used as cord; shields and sun-hats are also made from the stalk. ' Besides its cool, agreeable shade,' writes Mr. Stanley, ' the banana plant will supply a peasant of Uganda with bread, potatoes, dessert, wine, beer, medicine, house and fence, bed, cloth, cooking-pot, table-cloth, parcel wrapper, thread, cord, rope, sponge, bath, shield, sun-hat, even a canoe—in fact, almost everything but meat and iron. With the banana plant he is happy, fat, and thriving; without it, he is a famished, discontented, woe-begone wretch, hourly expecting death.'

After a stay of three months and five days with Mtesa, Stanley joined the expedition at Dumo, and found that Frank Pocock and the men had enjoyed excellent health. All this time they had been sustained free of cost by the emperor; so Stanley sent back his escort to Mtesa, with a present of four bales of cloth and 140 lbs. of choice beads.

Mtesa had sent Sambuzi, provided with an escort of over two thousand warriors, with the command to take Stanley to Lake Nyanza or Muta N'zige. The expedition was once more re-formed, the loads were re-packed, and the boats prepared for transport overland. An india-rubber pontoon previously in use was condemned, and its place was supplied by a new and light canoe, named the *Livingstone*. Seven days after his arrival at Dumo, Stanley began his march to the general rendezvous at the Katonga river, where they met with Sambuzi in command of King Mtesa's escort. Sambuzi proved dilatory in his movements, and was haughty in his demeanour. At Kawanga, on the frontier of Uganda, where the forces had been collected, the exploring army numbered 2800 strong. On 1st January 1876 the whole band filed out from under the plantain shades of Kawanga, each detachment being under the flag of its respective leader. Entering hostile Unyoro, the difference in the dwelling-places and in the food, as compared with Uganda, was at once apparent. Instead of living chiefly on bananas, their place was supplied by sweet potatoes and salt, and such other vegetables as could be readily obtained. On the 5th January, crossing the river Katonga, from the summit of a tall hill in Western Benga a faint view was obtained of an enormous blue mass afar off, which was called the Great Mountain, in the country of Gambaragara. In honour of one of the promoters of the expedition, Mr. Stanley named it the Gordon-Bennett.

In the neighbourhood of several villages in Southern Unyoro, several deep pits, with small circular mouths, were discovered, leading downwards to roomy excavations. The expedition camped on the banks of the Mpanga river on 8th January. This river, rising near the base of Mount Gordon-Bennett, flows east by Mount Edwin Arnold, unites with the Rasango river, and falls into Beatrice Gulf on the Muta N'zige. Ankori or Usagora was the next district entered. The nights grew colder, the thermometer fell, and fogs now prevailed. The march of 9th January brought them into a singularly wild and beautifully picturesque country— what Mr. Stanley has termed the Switzerland of Africa. By the 11th January they had sighted the lake. A panic seized hold of Mtesa's escort, however, and they showed decided symptoms of a wish to return. The warlike attitude of the tribes around the lake had fostered this desire. For thus attempting to turn back, Sambuzi was punished by Mtesa, after Stanley had remonstrated with him.

Returning, Stanley reached Kafurro in Karagwe, which owes its importance to being the seat of several rich Arab traders. In the neighbourhood is situated Chief Rumanika's village, which they visited. 'The sons of Rumanika,' writes Stanley, 'nourished on a milk diet, were in remarkably good condition. Their unctuous skins shone as though the tissues of fat beneath were dissolving in the heat, and their rounded bodies were as taut as a drumhead. Their eyes were large, and beaming and lustrous with life, yet softened by an extreme gentleness of expression. The sculptor might have obtained from any of these royal boys a dark model for another statue to rival the classic Antinous.' Mr. Stanley was charmed with the gentleness and tenderness of Rumanika. His face reminded him of a deep, still well, or of a Christian patriarch or saint of old, and the tones of his voice were calm. In this respect he was widely different from the impulsive Mtesa, whose eyes, when in a raging fit, were like 'balls of fire and large as fists,' and whose words were 'like gunpowder.' While staying here, a boat and canoe race was undertaken. On the day following Mr. Stanley sailed round the Windermere lake ; its extreme length, when at its fullest, is about eight miles, and its extreme breadth about two and a half. The six hot springs of Mtagata were also visited. These springs enjoy a great repute amongst invalids throughout the districts of Karagwe and the neighbouring countries. On returning to Rumanika's quarters, Stanley was treated to a good deal of geographical information of a fabulous character.

Rumanika possessed an armoury and museum, containing arms and curiosities. The armoury was a dome-shaped circular hut, about 30 feet in diameter, neatly thatched with straw. It contained amongst other things sixteen rude brass figures of ducks, with copper wings; ten representations of elands, and ten headless cows of copper; bill-hooks of iron, doubled-bladed spears, fly-flaps set in iron, and massive cleaver-looking knives. Some exquisite native cloths were as fine as cotton shirting, and were coloured black and red, in patterns and stripes. There were also drinking-cups, goblets, trenchers, and milk-dishes of wood. A revolving rifle, the gift of Captain Speke, had also an honoured place amongst the collection.

Bidding a regretful good-bye to Rumanika, and after a month's rest at Kafurro, the journey was resumed on the 26th

March. On the 27th, Mr. Stanley shot three rhinoceroses, which furnished supplies of meat for their journey through the wilderness of Uhimba. On entering Western Usui, there was a famine, and an extravagant amount of cloth had to be dealt out for four days' rations. On the 7th April the journey was continued in a southerly direction.

The following is Mr. Stanley's summary of progress made up till this time :—'From the 17th January 1875 up to 7th April 1876, we had been engaged in tracing the extreme southern sources of the Nile, from the marshy plains and cultivated uplands, where they are borne down to the mighty reservoir called the Victoria Nyanza. We had circumnavigated the entire expanse ; penetrated to every bay, inlet, and creek ; become acquainted with almost every variety of wild human nature—the mild and placable, the ferocious and impracticably savage, the hospitable and the inhospitable, the generous-souled as well as the ungenerous ; we had viewed their methods of war, and had witnessed them imbruing their hands in each other's blood with savage triumph and glee ; we had been five times sufferers by their lust for war and murder, and had lost many men through their lawlessness and ferocity ; we had travelled hundreds of miles to and fro on foot along the northern coast of the Victorian sea ; and, finally, had explored with a large force the strange countries lying between the two lakes, Muta N'zige and the Victoria, and had been permitted to gaze upon the arm of the lake named by me "Beatrice Gulf," and to drink of its sweet waters. We had then returned from further quest in that direction, unable to find a peaceful resting-place on the lake shores, and had struck south from the Katonga lagoon down to the Alexandra Nile, the principal affluent of the Victoria lake, which drains nearly all the waters from the west and south-west. We had made a patient survey of over one-half of its course, and then, owing to want of the means to feed the rapacity of the churlish tribes which dwell in the vicinity of the Alexandra Nyanza, and to our reluctance to force our way against the will of the natives, opposing unnecessarily our rifles to their spears and arrows, we had been compelled, on the 7th April, to bid adieu to the lands which supply the Nile, and to turn our faces towards the Tanganyika. . . . I have not ventured beyond the limits assigned me, viz. the exploration of the southern sources of the Nile, and the solution of the problem left unsolved by Speke and Grant, "Is the Victoria Nyanza one lake, or does it consist of five lakes, as reported by Livingstone, Burton, and others?" This problem has been satisfactorily solved, and Speke has now the full glory of having discovered the largest inland sea on the continent of Africa, also its principal affluent, as well as the outlet. I must also give him credit for having understood the geography of the countries he travelled through better than any of those who so persistently assailed his hypothesis; and I here record my admiration of the geographical genius that from mere native report first sketched with such a masterly hand the bold outlines of the Victoria Nyanza.'

Proceeding southwards towards Lake Tanganyika, a halt was made at Nyambarri. Here there was a rupture in the camp, caused by Msenna, one of the men, who endeavoured to bring about a revolt amongst the Wangwana and Wanyamwezi. Msenna was reduced from his former captaincy of ten men to the ranks. At Ndeverva, on the 18th April, the report reached them that the terrible chief Mirambo, the greatest king in Unyamwezi, was marching towards them. On the

following day they reached one of the largest villages in
Unyamwezi, called Serombo, when they heard that Mirambo
was expected there, but only on a visit to his friend Ndega.
The town-criers, preceded by the sound of iron bells, were
heard to make the following announcement :—

'Listen, O men of Serombo! Mirambo, the brother of
Ndega, cometh in the morning. Be ye prepared, therefore,
for his young men are hungry. Send your women to dig
potatoes! Mirambo cometh! Dig potatoes, potatoes; dig
potatoes, to-morrow!'

Stanley had an interview with Mirambo on 22d April 1876,
and found him the reverse of all his previous conceptions.
He is 'a man about 5 feet 11 inches in height, and about
thirty-five years old, with not an ounce of superfluous flesh
about him. A handsome, regular-featured, mild-voiced, soft-
spoken man, with what one might call a "mock" demeanour,
very generous and open-handed.' After exchanging presents
(those from Mirambo being particularly liberal), and perform-
ing the ceremony of blood-brotherhood, they parted the best
of friends. The demands made for tribute by the petty chiefs
of Unyamwezi were for the most part extortionate, and were
refused. Their eyes rested on Lake Tanganyika on 27th May
1876. At three o'clock in the afternoon of that day they were
in Ujiji. There was little change in the place since the
previous visit in 1871. The house where he and Livingstone
had lived was, however, burned down; and the hero who had
formerly filled the place with such absorbing interest was
gone.

During this visit, Stanley took the opportunity of describing
the place minutely. The port, he tells us, is divided into
two districts,—Ugoy, occupied by the Arabs; and Kawele,

inhabited by the Wangwana, slaves, and natives. The market-
place was smaller and more contracted than on his previous
visit.   On the beach before the market-place, the Arab canoes
are drawn up.   The commodities brought to the market consist of sweet potatoes, yams, sugar-canes, ground nuts, oil nuts,
palm-oil and palm-wine, butter, pombé, beans, fowls, goats,
broad-tailed sheep and sometimes oxen, tomatoes, plantains,
dried fish, etc.   The natives had begun to be extortionate in
their dealings, which proved rather exasperating to the Arabs.
Cloths, sheeting, and beads of various kinds was the currency
most commonly used.   The country of Ujiji extends along the
Tanganyika, between the Linche river, to a distance of forty-
five miles.   Its breadth is about twenty miles.   The king at
that time was called Mgassa, and resides amongst the mountains bordering upon Uguru.   Stanley estimated its population
at about 36,000 souls.

Before proceeding to explore Lake Tanganyika in the *Lady
Alice*, Stanley was much disappointed to find that his letters
had not been forwarded as he had desired by the Governor of
Unyanyembe.   Observations taken during the voyage proved
unmistakeably that the waters of the lake were rising.   In
time it may overflow its banks by way of the Lukuga creek.
'When the Tanganyika,' he writes, ' has risen three feet higher,
there will be no surf at the mouth of the Lukuga, no silt of
sand, no oozing mud-banks, no rush-covered old river-course ;
but the accumulated waters of over a hundred rivers will
sweep through the ancient gap with the force of a cataclysm,
bearing away on its flood all the deposits of organic debris at
present in the Lukuga creek, down the steep incline, to swell
the tribute due to the mighty Livingstone.'   Stanley arrived at
Ujiji after being absent fifty-one days, and having sailed 810

miles. The entire coast-line of the Tanganyika he proved to be 930 miles. Frank Pocock, who had been left in charge of the camp, was exceedingly glad to see his master return, as he had been down several times with severe attacks of fever. Five of his Wangwana men were also dead from small-pox, and six others were seriously ill. The pest of small-pox spread dismay in the camp.

On 25th August the order was given to march, when it was found that 38 out of 170 men had deserted. After crossing the Tanganyika there were other desertions. Seven of the deserters were secured by Francis Pocock and a native, and punished as a warning to the others. Mr. Stanley here takes the liberty of moralizing on Dr. Livingstone's last expedition. He was left at one time with but seven men out of seventy; had he shown greater firmness, fewer desertions might have taken place, and six good years, and finally his life, might have been saved. While journeying to Manyema, the following remarks on Stanley's character, and the purpose of his mission, were reported to him by a young Arab :—' Kassanga, chief of Ruanda, says, " How can the white men be good when they come for no trade, whose feet one never sees, who always go covered from head to foot with clothes? Do not tell me they are good and friendly. There is something very mysterious about them; perhaps wicked. Probably they are magicians; at any rate, it is better to leave them alone, and to keep close until they are gone."' Crossing a ridge, forming the boundary between Uguha and Ubujwe, they found the country abounding in forests and fruit-trees. Honey and buffalo were also plentiful. The natives of Rua, Uguha, and Ubujwe were found to be adepts in the art of hair-dressing. Carved statues in wood are also not uncommon.

Uhyeya was the district adjoining Ubujwe, which they found peopled by natives rather lower in the scale of humanity. They were partial to ochre, black paints, and a composition of black mud, which they moulded into the form of a plate and stuck on the back of their heads. They were, however, very ready in supplying the wants of the explorer. Uvinza, the next district which he traversed, consisted of several square miles, and led to Uhombo, a district of remarkable fertility. The natives were very willing to trade, and supplied them with palm-butter for cooking, sugar-cane, goats, chickens, sweet potatoes, bananas, plantain and palm wines, and good water.

Marching from Uhombo, Riba-Riba, a frontier village of Manyema, was reached on 5th October. Here the form of the huts, instead of being conical as formerly, was square, with gradually sloping roof, wattled and plastered with mud. Nature, in the Manyema district, was on a splendid scale; the valleys and hill-sides were clothed with a profuse and robust vegetation. 'Her grasses,' says Mr. Stanley, 'are coarse, and wound like knives and needles; her reeds are tough, and tall as bamboos; her creepers and convolvuli are of cable thickness and length; her thorns are hooks of steel; her trees shoot up to a height of a hundred feet. We find no pleasure in straying in search of wild flowers, and game is left undisturbed because of the difficulty of moving about; for, once the main path is left, we find ourselves overhead amongst thick, tough, unyielding, lacerating grass.'

Leaving Riba-Riba, Ka Bambarre was reached, where traces of Dr. Livingstone still existed amongst the natives. Mats were spread under a palm tree, and the following conversation took place :—

'Did you know the old white man? Was he your father?'

' He was not my father ; but I knew him well.'

' Eh, do you hear that ?' he asked his people. ' He says he knew him. Was he not a good man ?'

' Yes, very good.'

' You say well. He was good to me, and he saved me from the Arabs many a time. The Arabs are hard men ; and often he would step between them and me when they were hard on me. He was a good man, and my children were fond of him. I hear he is dead ?'

' Yes ; he is dead.'

' Where has he gone to ?'

' Above, my friend,' said Stanley, pointing to the sky.

' Ah !' said he breathlessly, and looking up. ' Did he come from above ?'

' No ; but good men like him go above when they die.'

The people here, of an Ethiopic-negro type, were more refined and better looking than those of the Uhombo district. Their weapons are a short sword scabbarded with wood, and a spear. Their dress consisted of a narrow apron of antelope-skin or grass cloth. Patches of mud were attached to their beards, back hair, and behind the ears. Some had their entire head crowned with mud. The women sometimes manufactured their hair, with a stiffening of light cane, into a bonnet-shaped head-dress, with the back hair loose and flowing to their waist. They also do the heaviest amount of work, the fishing and agriculture.

' The houses,' says Mr. Stanley, ' are separated into two or more apartments, and, on account of the compact nature of the clay and tamped floor, are easily kept clean. The roofs are slimy with the reek of smoke, as though they had been painted with coal-tar. The household chattels or furniture are limited to food baskets, earthenware pots, an assortment of wickerwork dishes, the family shields, spears, knives, swords, and tools, and the fish baskets lying outside. They are tolerably hospitable, and permit strangers the free use of their dwellings. The bananas and plantains are very luxuriant, while the Guinea-palms supply the people with oil and wine; the forests give them fuel, the rivers fish, and the gardens cassava, ground nuts, and Indian corn.' The Luama river was crossed on the 11th on the western side; the women fled at the approach of the caravan. The asses of the expedition were the first seen in Manyema, and attracted great attention. Livingstone and Cameron, after crossing the Luama, had proceeded westward; Stanley decided to follow the river to its junction with the Lualaba. Kabungwe was reached on the 13th; beyond this place he found the country extremely populous. At Mtuyu, the easternmost settlement of the country of Uzura, the people pretended that the small-pox had done away with the population. Near Mpungu, fifteen miles west of Mtuyu, dwelt a tribe with remarkable beards; the chief, Kitete, was ornamented with one which was plaited and decorated at the tips with blue glass beads, and was 20 inches long. Four miles from Mpungu was seen the confluence of the Luama with the Lualaba. The Luama appeared to be about 400 yards broad at the mouth, and the Lualaba was about 1400 yards wide, winding south and by east, and of a pale grey colour. The young explorer was filled with rapture at the sight. After following one of the affluents, he had now arrived at the great river whose unknown course he was about to determine and settle for ever, by following it to the ocean. Reaching Mwana Mamba's district, Stanley heard from Hamed bin Mohammed, or Tippu Tib, a gentleman Arab who had

escorted Lieutenant Cameron across the Lualaba as far as
Utstera, that the reason why he had not proceeded farther in
that direction was the want of canoes and the hostility of the
savages. Dr. Livingstone was deterred in somewhat the same
way. After debating the matter, whether he would go forward,
and hearing what the Arabs had to tell about the Lualaba,—
that it flowed north, and still north,—an agreement was drawn
up with Tippu Tib. It was to the effect that he would
receive one hundred and forty guns and seventy Wanyamwezi
spearmen; these were to escort the expedition a distance of
sixty camps. If the countries were found to be hostile, and if
without hopes of meeting other traders, they should all return
to Nyangwe. Ration money to last for ten days was then
counted to Tippu Tib, and the expedition started from
Mwana Mamba on the 24th October. After a journey of
twelve miles through a fine rolling country, they encamped at
Kankumba on the 25th; Nyangwe was but five miles distant.
The grass of this neighbourhood was 8 feet high, with stalks
an inch in diameter, and looking like 'a waving country
planted with young bamboo.'

The expedition was in excellent marching order when
Nyangwe was reached on the 27th October. This is the
westernmost Arab settlement reached by the traders from
Zanzibar, and stands in longitude 26° 16', south latitude 4° 15',
on the east side of the Lualaba.

Tippu Tib had reached Nyangwe on the 2d November with
a force of nearly seven hundred people. About three hundred
of these men were to be sent to a country called Tatta, to the
east of Usongora Meno. The total number of men, women,
and children connected with the expedition was 154. The
arms were as follows:—29 Sniders, 32 percussion-lock muskets,

2 Winchesters, 2 double-barrelled guns, 10 revolvers, 68 axes.
The men, to the number of 250, who were to accompany the
expedition a distance of sixty camps, are Arabs, half-castes,
Wangwana, 100 Wanyamwezi, Ruga-Ruga, armed with spears,
bows and arrows, and only some of them possessing flint-locks.
In addition there are about fifty youths, from ten to eighteen
years of age, who will be employed as gun-bearers, house
servants, cooks, carpenters, house-builders, blacksmiths, etc.
Hopefully the young explorer and his men started from
Nyangwe, westwards, to explore the nine hundred miles of
country unknown to Europeans.

The expedition was marching through the forest of Mitamba
on the 6th November. The path through this twilight forest
was gloomy in the extreme, the damp moisture dropping from
the leaves, and making the pathway into pasty mud. The
growth of tangled underwood, too, was immense. Ditches
had to be crossed, and the travellers were being continually
tormented by the creepers and climbing plants which obstructed the pathway. The atmosphere was stifling; a damp,
hot steam was rising from the moist earth, and the clothes of
the travellers were saturated with moisture. 'It was crawling,
scrambling, tearing through the damp, dank jungles, and such
height and depth of woods.' The men who carried the boat,
which was in sections, complained bitterly of fatigue when they
reached Mpotira. Kimssi, in Uregga, the forest country, was
reached on the 10th. The Waregga, the natives of that
district, although living secluded lives, could boast of a fair
amount of comfort in their dwelling-places. Their villages
consist of long rows of houses connected together, and from
50 to 300 yards in length. The doorways in the walls are
only 2 feet square, and cut at about 18 inches above ground.

These blocks are divided into separate apartments, in the interior, for the respective families. The pipe and various medicinal herbs are stuck in the roof. Various skins of animals helped to make up the household furniture also. Cane settees, capable of seating three persons comfortably, were also not uncommon. A bench 4 or 5 feet long, cut out of a single log of wood, also formed an article of furniture. The males wear skull-caps of goat or monkey skin. In the case of the chiefs and elders, this was exchanged for leopard skin. The women decorate their arms and legs very lavishly with iron and copper rings.

The march of the 15th was full of troubles, and extended over six miles and a half. Mr. Stanley's shoes were worn out, and half the march was performed with naked feet. His last pair were drawn from the store and put on. Frank Pocock did the same. The courage of the men was much daunted because of the difficulties of the way. Amongst the animals seen on the march were a python 10 feet long, a green viper, a puff adder, a lemur, and many different species of monkeys and baboons. The undergrowth, which rendered locomotion almost impossible, is thus described by Mr. Stanley:—'It consisted of ferns, spear-grass, water-cane, and orchidaceous plants, mixed with wild vines, cable thicknesses of the *Ficus elastica,* and a sprinkling of mimosas, acacias, tamarinds, lliams, palms of various species, wild date, *Ralphia vinifera,* the elais, the fan, rattans, and a hundred other varieties, all struggling for every inch of space, and swarming upward with a luxuriance and density that only this extraordinary hothouse atmosphere could nourish. We had certainly seen forests before, but this scene was an epoch in our lives ever to be remembered for its bitterness; the gloom enhanced the dismal

misery of our life; the slopping moisture, the unhealthy
reeking atmosphere, and the monotony of the scenes; nothing
but the eternal interlaced branches, the tall aspiring stems,
rising from a tangle through which we had to. burrow and
crawl like wild animals, on hands and feet.' At the next
halting-place, Wane-Kirumbu, Tippu Tib, the Arab leader,
expressed a wish to return, but after much solicitation he
agreed to march twenty camps farther from that place. The
present of fifteen cowries to the chief of Wane-Kirumbu was
received with emotions of lively gratitude. A large native
forge employing about a dozen native smiths was at work
here. They manufactured broad-bladed spears, and broad
knives of all sizes.

The village of Kampunzu was reached on the 17th
November. Two rows of skulls 10 feet apart, imbedded
about two inches in the ground, ran along the entire length of
the village. The skulls were one hundred and eighty-six in
number, but they were informed that they were those of 'sokos,'
or chimpanzees from the forest. Two of these skulls brought
to England were examined by Professor Huxley, and pro-
nounced to be those of the ordinary African negro. The
conclusion to be drawn from this is that the people of
Kampunzu may be cannibals. These Wavinzi warriors are
armed with short broad-bladed spears and small bows, with
arrows dipped in vegetable poison. In the use of the latter
they are very dexterous, sending an arrow easily 200 yards.
The men wore skins of civet or monkey in back and front,
with the tails downward. The women wore narrow aprons of
bark or grass cloth. A march of five miles brought them to
the Lualaba, in south latitude 3° 35', east longitude 25° 49'.
From this point he decided to drop the name Lualaba, and

call it the Livingstone. They encamped on the banks of the river, which was here 1200 yards wide. Watching the river flowing gently past, he was now more than ever determined to make it his pathway westward. It would at least be better than the trackless forests of which they had already had such experience. On the 20th the whole expedition had crossed the river and encamped in one of the villages of the Wenya. The natives, frightened at this sudden incursion, had all disappeared into the bush on the following morning. The natives behaved in the same manner in several villages through which they passed. On the 23d November they halted at the Ruiki river. The natives here took the opportunity of attacking Stanley's party while he was absent exploring the Ruiki. The expedition now proceeded down the river, when the rapids of Ukassa were reached. On the 29th, Mburri, on the left bank, was reached, and the journey downwards was continued on the following day. Two finely-wooded islands in mid-stream were passed, and a halt was made at the market-place of Usako Ngongo. On 1st December, Ukongeh, opposite Mitandeh island, was reached. On the 4th, they reached Muriwa creek, on the north bank of which was a series of villages, having one broad uniform street, thirty feet wide and two miles in length. This town was called Ikondee, but all the natives had fled at their approach, leaving their fine gardens of bananas, melons, sugar-cane, ground nuts, and plantations of cassava, at the mercy of the stranger. As many of the men were here suffering from diseases brought on by the fatigues and troubles of the march, a canoe was procured and constructed to be used as a floating hospital. A Watwa dwarf was captured in the woods, with a bow and a quiver of poisoned arrows in his hand. On the 8th December, moving down the river to Unya-N'singe, they discovered that it was a large town about a mile in length. The natives here, the Wasongora Mono, attacked the expedition in fourteen canoes, but they were promptly repulsed with considerable loss.

Still gliding down the river, Kisui Kachiambi was reached on the 14th, which was found to consist of three hundred long houses, and to be about a mile in length. A well-planned attack by the natives was frustrated, as the expedition was thoroughly prepared. Descending the stream on the 18th, showers of arrows were discharged at them from the jungle. Refuge was taken behind a stockade which was hastily prepared at Vinya-Njara; here they protected themselves as they best could from the showers of arrows and spears launched at them. Refuge was next taken in a deserted village lower down the river. Each end of the village was defended. About noon one day a huge flotilla of canoes was discovered, manned by between five and eight hundred men, coming down the river to attack them. The war-horns were sounded, and every man within the village prepared for the attack. At last they were beaten off, with great loss, the arrival of Tippu Tib with the land division helping this consummation. They took shelter farther down the river. The loss to the expedition consisted of four men killed and thirteen wounded. In a night expedition, over thirty canoes were captured from the natives. In the terms of agreement afterwards made, twenty-three of these canoes were retained, and the ceremony of blood-brotherhood was performed between Safeni and the chief of Vinya-Njara.

After this engagement, discouraged, and daily growing weaker because of the number of deaths, the Arab leaders, Tippu Tib, Sheikh Abdallah, and Muini Ibrahim, declared their intention of returning by another route to Nyangwe. Their contract was not yet fulfilled, but Mr. Stanley felt that their courage was exhausted. Gifts were distributed, and an assurance was asked from Tippu Tib that he would use his influence to get the principal men of the expedition to follow him in his further explorations. This he promised to do. Stanley then addressed his followers thus :—

‘Into whichever sea this great river empties, there shall we follow it. You have seen that I have saved you a score of times, when everything looked black and dismal for us. That care of you to which you owe your safety hitherto, I shall maintain until I have seen you safe and sound in your own homes, and under your own palm trees. All I ask of you is, perfect trust in whatever I say. On your lives depends my own ; if I risk yours, I risk mine. As a father looks after his children, I will look after you. It is true we are not so strong as when the Wanyaturu attacked us, or when we marched through Unyoro to Muta N’zige, but we are of the same band of men, and we are still of the same spirit. Many of our party have already died, but death is the end of all; and if they died earlier than we, it was the will of God, and who shall rebel against His will ? It may be, we shall meet a hundred wild tribes yet, who, for the sake of eating us, will rush to meet and fight us. We have no wish to molest them. We have monies with us, and are, therefore, not poor. If they fight us, we must accept it as an evil, like disease, which we cannot help. We shall continue to do our utmost to make friends, and the river is wide and deep. If we fight, we fight for our lives. It may be that we shall be distressed by famine and want. It may be that we shall meet with many more cataracts, or find ourselves before a great lake, whose wild

waves we cannot cross with these canoes; but we are no
children, we have heads and arms, and are we not always
under the eye of God, who will do with us as He sees fit?
Therefore, my children, make up your minds, as I have made
up mine, that as we are now in the very middle of this
continent, and it would be just as bad to return as to go on,
that we shall continue our journey, that we shall toil on and
on, by this river and no other, to the salt sea.' This speech
awakened considerable enthusiasm amongst the men, and
preparations were proceeded with at once.

On Christmas Day 1876, the men were mustered and
appointed to their respective canoes. The rest of the day was
spent in festivity, in canoe races, and in foot races. On the
following day, Tippu Tib gave a feast of rice and roasted
sheep to the members of the expedition, which helped to
prolong and maintain their cheerful feelings and prospects
of success. After pulling up stream and camping on an
island all night, they prepared to leave Vinya-Njara for ever
on the morning of the 28th December. A dense mist hung
over the river in the morning, which slowly lifting, the order
to embark was given. As the canoes were descending past
where Tippu Tib and his men were encamped, they heard
them joining in a farewell song. As the notes of the song
floated towards them, the leader and his men were well-nigh
overcome. 'Louder the sad notes swelled on our ears,' he
writes, 'full of a pathetic and mournful meaning. With
bated breath we listened to the rich music, which spoke to us
unmistakeably of parting, of sundered friendship, a long,
perhaps an eternal farewell. We came in view of them, as,
ranged along the bank in picturesque costumes, the sons of
Unyamwezi sang their last song. We waved our hands to

them. Our hearts were so full of grief that we could not speak. Steadily the brown flood bore us by, and fainter and fainter came the notes down the water, till finally they died away, leaving us all alone in our loneliness.' A halt was made that day at Kali-Karero, where the natives were peace-ably inclined. Fourteen different villages were passed that day, a proof that the Vinya-Njara district was very populous. Next day, in passing down the river, big wooden drums were beaten, which told of the presence of the stranger, and the natives on the right bank gave them such a salutation as clearly proved they were cannibals. ' Meat ! meat ! ah ! ha ! We shall have plenty of meat ! Bo—bo—bo—bo ! Bo—bo —bo—bo—o—o !' A show of fight cleared the river of these savages. On 29th December they encamped on an unin-habited spot opposite Vina-Kya. The savages manned their drums and canoes, and advanced towards them. The two interpreters belonging to the expedition did their best to prove to them that their errand was a peaceful one. They were beaten off for that day. The mouth of the Low-wa or Row-wa river now came into view ; its mouth, where it emptied itself into the Livingstone, was a thousand yards wide. The right bank of the Livingstone, at the mouth of the Low-wa, had no appearance of being inhabited. The undergrowth to be witnessed there seemed impenetrable. ' Entomologists and naturalists,' he says, ' might revel there.' The following animals abounded :—Myriapedes, brown, black, and yellow ants, the mautis, the earth caterpillar, the ladybird, and countless insects. Mr. Stanley dissipates the idea of a primeval forest being silent. ' The hum and murmur of hundreds of busy insect tribes,' he writes, ' make populous the twilight shadows that reign under the primeval growth. I hear the grinding of millions of mandibles, the furious hiss of a tribe just alarmed or about to rush to battle, millions of tiny wings rustling through the nether air, the march of an insect tribe under the leaves, the startling leap of an awakened mautis, the chirp of some eager and garrulous cricket, the buzz of an ant-lion, the roar of a bull-frog. Add to these the crackle of twigs, the fall of leaves, the dropping of nut and berry, the occasional crash of a branch, or the constant creaking and swaying of the forest tops as the strong wind brushes them or the gentle breezes awake them to whispers.' The night of 30th December was spent in the leafy shelter opposite the Low-wa confluence. The natives, who sold them ten gigantic plantains, 13 inches long and 3 inches in diameter, informed them that they were encamped on the shore of the Lulu, an uninhabited portion of the territory of Wanpuma. They crossed to the Iryamba side of the Livingstone.. A strong breeze had arisen, when two men were drowned by the upsetting of a canoe, and four muskets and a sackful of beads were lost. On the following day the journey was continued. The first day of 1877 began while passing an uninhabited tract, and Stanley found time to ruminate and enjoy the forest beauty and stillness without being troubled with thoughts of the past or future. Sounds of war-drums were, however, heard early that day, both from an island in the river and from its banks. The word Seu-neu-neh, or peace, was shouted out in vain. The reply was, 'We shall eat Wajiwa meat to-day. Oho, we shall eat Wajiwa meat.' The natives were beaten back, however, and progress was resumed. On 3d January they glided down to Kankore, the word Seu-neu-neh being all the while shouted out. The natives gathered on the banks in a more peaceful attitude, and presents of beads were given to two women who had the courage to paddle out towards them to treat with them. The men, like the natives of Waregga, were tattooed and similarly dressed; the women wore bits of carved wood and necklaces; polished iron rings were used as armlets and leg ornaments.

Leaving Kankore, the savages of Mwana Ntaba disturbed their further progress, and alarmed their brethren on the right bank. These natives were in full war-paint, one-half of their bodies being white, the other half red, with broad black bars. In their first attack, a canoe 85 feet 3 inches long was captured from them. About forty canoes were seen making down stream, evidently bent on mischief. Passing the mouth of a river about 200 yards wide, Mr. Stanley named it the Leopold river, after Leopold II., king of the Belgians. Soon after passing this river, the roar of the first cataract of the Stanley Fall series was heard. But the roar of the savages from either side of the river resounded even more loudly than the noise of the cataract. In an encounter on 5th January, the Mwana Ntaba were repulsed, with a loss to Stanley of two men wounded and two killed. The bodies of the latter were committed to the Livingstone, in order that they might not become the food of the cannibals. By the afternoon of the 8th they were beyond the first cataract, and at anchor in a creek between Baswa island and the left bank. Another encounter with natives took place on the 11th, farther down the river, and when opposite to Ntunduru island. Three of his men made a narrow escape from drowning just above the second cataract, and were rescued from a small islet just above the falls in a very remarkable manner. A sharp encounter and some clever manœuvring with the cannibals of Asama island led to peace, when the expedition was well supplied with bananas. Beyond the fifth cataract, and north of Asama, the river widened out to a breadth of 2000 yards. Encamping on the 19th at Wane-Mpungu, in the morning it was discovered that a tall high net surrounded the camp. The net was cut, an ambuscade was laid, when eight of the Wane-Mpungu were captured. The upper teeth of each of these savages were filed, two carved rows of tattoo marks were on their foreheads, and their temples were punctured. On being questioned, they confessed that they had been lying in wait for man-meat. These captives accompanied Stanley in his examination of the river, and were set at liberty on the right bank. The next camping stage was above the sixth cataract, near an island thickly peopled by a tribe of the Waregga called Wana-Rukura. The natives were troublesome here. On the 20th they halted on a large island which had been deserted by the Wana-Rukura; and by noon of the 23d they had cleared the sixth cataract without accident. Above the seventh cataract an island was discovered peopled by the Wenya, who, after some hostilities, deserted their villages. The population of this cluster of villages was estimated by Mr. Stanley at about 6000. The river above the seventh cataract is 1300 yards wide; contracted to a narrow space between the island of Wenya and the steep banks opposite, it ' rushes with resistless speed for a few hundred yards, and then falls about ten feet into a boiling and tumultuous gulf, wherein are lines of brown waves six feet high leaping with terrific bounds, and hurling themselves against each other in dreadful fury.' Fish were abundant in the neighbourhood of the falls; the natives are in the habit of entrapping them in fish-baskets. The Wenya seemed to be industrious; many of them possessed large wooden chests, in which were preserved their treasures of beads and berries, oyster and mussel shells. The paddles were made out of wood resembling mahogany; and cord made of hyphene palm and banana fibre was also found there. Earthenware jars were in every house. By the 28th of January, Stanley and his men were entirely clear of the falls, which had occupied them twenty-two days, during which time they had been continually beset by the savage denizens of the fastnesses on the route.

All the members of the expedition were now in good spirits, as they cleared the falls and hastened down the river into open water. Frank Pocock cheered himself by the singing of several hymns, which the leader of the expedition thought were scarcely bright enough for the occasion. On the 28th, the Mburra, a fine river 300 yards wide, was passed; and a mile below this confluence they encamped first at Ukobia island, and then at Usembi. Farther down the river, at Ituka, the expedition had its twenty-fifth encounter with natives since leaving the Ruiki river. Sixty-five large shields had been taken in these encounters, which were of great service, as they were held up by the women and children before the fighting men. These shields were impervious against spears and arrows, and enabled the gunners to do deadly execution. In order to frighten the natives who were annoying the expedition, opposite Yangambi a capture was made. The captive explained that the river at that point was called Izangi; the settlements on the right bank were in the country of Kovuru; the country on the left bank he called Yambarri. The river below Yangambi had grown from 3000 to 4000 yards wide. Islands were also getting more numerous. Coming in view of the market-place of Avuwimi on 1st February, scores of canoes rushed out against the intruders. Passing the mouth of a vast

affluent called the Avuwimi, 340 miles north of Nyangwe, and
about 2000 yards wide, a number of canoes were also seen
hovering about the islets in the centre of the river. Coming
in view of the right branch of the affluent, and looking up
stream, an immense concourse of canoes were seen to be
bearing down upon them. Orders were given to anchor the
canoes in line, about ten yards apart; the *Lady Alice* was
moved upwards, and anchored fifty yards above them. The
fighting men in the boats were well defended by a line of
shields held up by the non-combatants—men, women, and
children. A monster canoe led the attack, when it was discovered that there were fifty-four in all. Forty men were
rowing on each side in the large canoe; ten young warriors
stood in the bow, adorned with a head-dress of crimson and
grey parrot's feathers; eight men guided the vessel at the
stern with paddles, the tops of which were tipped with ivory;
ten men, apparently chiefs, moved up and down the vessel.
The heads of all the natives bore a feather crown. Drums
were beaten, horns were sounded, and two thousand throats
sent forth a wild chant while preparing for the onset.

Stanley felt that the supreme hour was arrived, when it
would be death or victory. They resolved to sell their lives as
dearly as possible. He addressed his people thus : ' Boys, be
firm as iron; wait until you see the first spear, and then take
good aim. Don't fire all at once. Keep aiming until you are
sure of your man. Don't think of running away, for only your
guns can save you.' After five minutes' firing, the enemy was
obliged to re-form above the *Lady Alice.* Lifting their anchors,
they pursued them up stream, and did not halt until they had
chased them to the woods, which sheltered them from the
wrath of their pursuers. In the principal village ivory was as

'abundant as fuel;' and in a native temple built of this material, an idol, four feet high, painted with camwood dye,— a bright vermilion,—and with black eyes and beard and hair, was discovered. The roof of the temple was supported by thirty-three tusks of ivory. These were seized by the Wang-wana. One hundred other pieces of ivory were removed. Some of these pieces were in the shape of war-horns, ivory pestles for pounding cassava and other herbs, ivory armlets and balls, and ivory mallets for beating fig-bark into cloth.

Mr. Stanley gives a full inventory of the other commodities and articles found in this African village. ' The stores of beautifully-carved paddles, ten feet in length, some of which were iron-pointed; the enormous six-feet-long spears, which were designed more for ornament than use; the splendid long knives, like Persian kummars, and bright iron-mounted sheaths, with broad belts of red buffalo and antelope hide; barbed spears, from the light assegai to the heavy double-handed sword-spear; the tweezers, hammers, prickers, hole-burners, hair-pins, fish-hooks, hammers, arm and leg rings of iron and copper; iron beads and wrist-bands; iron bells, axes, war-hatchets, adzes, hoes, dibbers, etc., proved the people on the banks of this river to be clever, intelligent, and more advanced in the arts than any hitherto observed since we commenced our descent of the Livingstone. The architecture of their huts, however, was the same, except the conical structure they had erected over their idol. Their canoes were much larger than those of the Mwana Ntaba, above the Stanley Falls, which had crocodiles and lizards carved on them. Their skull-caps of basket-work, leopard, civet, and monkey skins were similar to those that we had observed in Uregga. Their shields were like those of the Wariwa. There were various specimens of

African wood-carving in great and small idols, stools of ingenious pattern, double benches, walking-staffs, spear-staffs, paddles, flutes, grain-mortars, mallets, drums, clubs, troughs, scoops and canoe-balers, porridge spoons, etc. Gourds also exhibited taste in ornamentation. Their earthenware was very superior, their pipes of an unusual pattern—in short, everything that is of use to a well-found African village exhibited remarkable intelligence and prosperity. Evidences of cannibalism were numerous in the human 'soko' skulls that grinned on many poles, and the bones that were freely scattered in the neighbourhood, near the village garbage-heaps and the river banks, where one might suppose hungry canoemen to have enjoyed a cold collation on an ancient matron's arm. The most positive and downright evidence, in my opinion, of this hideous practice, was the thin forearm of a person that was picked up near a fire, with certain scorched ribs which might have been tossed into the fire after being gnawed.'

After receiving the waters of the Aruwimi, the great river broadened out to a great width, with from three to six branches, separated from each other by a series of islands. As they floated down between the islands, they had glimpses of several villages on their course. These islands were clothed with the wood indigenous to the tropics—teak and cotton-wood, the hyphene, borassus, wild date, and Guinea oil-palms, the rattan, the mangrove, and the shea butter-tree. The undergrowth was luxuriant, and grapes flourished by the river's bank. The terrors of the journey were still numerous,—the cataract and the whirling pool, the sudden storm blowing up the river, and the continual howling from either bank of the wrathful natives. On 8th February, the expedition was reduced to terrible straits for want of food. The three asses belonging to them were looked upon as well-nigh doomed. At the village of Rubunga, however, by tact and dexterity, Mr. Stanley succeeded in winning the natives over sufficiently to sell them bananas and fish. The chief of Rubunga, on being questioned as to the name of the river, replied that it was Ikutu ya Kongo. This confirmed Stanley's previous impression, since leaving the Stanley Falls, that they were sailing down the Congo.

The wearied members of the expedition encamped and rested at Rubunga, and a market was held for their benefit on 9th February. From the district around the natives arrived, bringing fresh and dried fish, snails, oysters, mussels, dried dog-meat, live dogs and goats, bananas, plantains, robes of grass cloth, cassava tubers, flour, and bread; spears, knives, axes, hatchets, bells, iron bracelets, and girdles—everything 'saleable or purchasable on the shores of the Livingstone.' Many of the knives were of a sickle-shaped pattern; the principal men carried weapons with brass handles. The Warua and Waguha wore their hair in tufts on the back of the head, fashioned with elegantly-shaped iron hair-pins. Their whole bodies are punctured and tattooed. Their breasts were marked with every conceivable design. The temple and cheek were also adorned with wavy lines. Their necklaces consisted of human, gorilla, and crocodile teeth. Some wore polished boars' tusks. Four ancient Portuguese muskets discovered amongst them strengthened the idea that the river really communicated with the coast.

On the 10th February, Urangi was reached, but the reception they received was very doubtful, and they found the natives great thieves. On leaving they were made the subject of a treacherous attack, but the expedition escaped amongst the windings of the creeks in the river. Below Rubunga the islands were much more numerous, producing great varieties of the palm species. Below Ukaturaka the river broadened out until it was about seven miles across. On the islands in the river, the elephant, the red buffalo, baboons, and long-tailed monkeys were seen. The channels swarmed with hippopotamus, crocodile, and the monitor. On the 13th February, they were attacked by the warriors of Marunja, whose war-cry was ' Yaha-ha-ha.' Stanley, seated in the bow of the *Lady Alice*, was repeatedly aimed at, nine bright musket barrels being levelled at him at once, only the curiosity and awe inspired by the sight of his white face, and by his dress, had prevented them from shooting him. The sight of their asses was also a matter of great wonder to them.

One of the most determined fights experienced on the river took place with the Bangala natives on the 14th February. In floating down the river, the usual war signal was given— drums were beaten, guns were loaded, spears and broadswords were being sharpened, in order to give a bloody welcome to the intruders. We must leave Mr. Stanley to tell this desperate encounter in his own words.

Standing up in his boat, Stanley endeavoured to conciliate them by holding out towards them a long piece of red cloth in one hand, and a coil of brass wire in another. ' I observed,' he says, ' three or four canoes approaching Frank's vessel with a most suspicious air about them, and several of their crews menacing him, at which Frank (Pocock) stood up and menaced them with his weapon. I thought the act premature, and ordered him to sit down and look away from them. I again raised the crimson cloth and wire, and, by pantomime, offered to give it to those in front, whom I was previously addressing; but almost immediately those natives who had threatened Frank fired into my boat, wounding three of my young crew—Mambu, Murabo, and Joffrai ; and two more natives fired into Frank's canoe, wounding two—Hatib and Muftah. The missiles fired into us were jagged pieces of iron and copper ore, precisely similar to those which the Ashantees employed. After this murderous outrage, there was no effort made to secure peace. The shields were lifted, and proved capital defences against the hail of slugs. Boat, shields, and canoes were pitted, but only a few shields were perforated. The conflict began in earnest, and lasted so long that ammunition had to be redistributed. We perceived that as the conflict continued every village sent out its quota. About two o'clock a canoe advanced with a swaggering air, its crew evidently intoxicated, and fired at us when within thirty yards. The boat instantly swept down to it and captured it, but the crew sprang into the river, and, being capital swimmers, were saved by a timely arrival of their friends. At three o'clock I counted sixty-three opposed to us. Some of the Bangala— which they disclosed themselves by their peculiar cries, " Yaha-ha-ha, ya Bangala !" " Ya Bangala, yaha-ha-ha !" — distinguished themselves by an audacity and courage that, for our own sakes, I was glad to see was not general ; especially one young chief, distinguished by his head-dress of white goat-skin, and a short mantle of the same material, and wreaths of thick brass wire on neck, arms, and legs, sufficient, indeed, to have protected those parts from slugs, and proving him to be a man of consequence. His canoe mates were ten in number, and his steersman, by his adroitness and dexterity, managed the canoe so well that after he and his mates had fired their guns, he instantly presented its prow and only a thin line of upright figures to our aim. Each time he dashed up to deliver his fire, all the canoes of his countrymen seemed stimulated by his example to emulate him. And, allowing five guns on an average to each of the sixty-three canoes, there were 315 muskets opposed to our 44. Their mistake was in supposing their slugs to have the same penetrative effect and long range as our missiles had. Only a few of the boldest approached after they had experienced our fire within a hundred yards. The young chief already mentioned frequently charged to within fifty yards, and delivered a smashing charge of missiles, almost all of which were either too low or too high. Finally, Manwa Sera wounded him with a Snider bullet in the thigh. The brave fellow coolly, and in presence of us all, took a piece of cloth and deliberately bandaged it, and then calmly retreated towards shore. This action was so noble and graceful that orders were given to let him withdraw unmolested. After his departure the firing became desultory, and at 5.30 P.M. our antagonists retired, leaving us to attend to our wounded, and to give three hearty cheers at our success. This was our thirty-first fight on the terrible river, the last but one, and certainly the most determined conflict that we had endured.' The huts of these savage warriors stretched about ten miles on the river side, at intervals of a mile or half a mile. Their principal trade was in ivory, and the river Bangala flows into the Congo from a northerly direction. The two white men of the expedition, Mr. Stanley and Frank Pocock, enjoyed better health on the river than they had done on any previous part of the journey.

While descending the left bank of the Livingstone, a large river emptying its waters into it was discovered, the mouth of which was over a thousand yards wide, the current of which was strong and deep, and of the colour of black tea. The natives of Ikengo called it the Ikelemba river. At this time they were in a great strait for food, any of the natives they had passed steadily refusing to supply it. Their wants were supplied at Ikengo, however, on 19th February. The natives held a market for their benefit on the 20th, when abundance of black pigs, goats, sheep, bananas, plantains, cassava, bread, flour, maize, sweet potatoes, yams, and fish were to be had. Passing the shores of Ubangi, the natives fired at them, but the width of the river and the number of channels by which they could escape rendered their hostilities harmless. The islets which they now passed were inexpressibly grateful to them, as they were unpeopled, and after the hard fighting they had endured, and the constant watchfulness which they were obliged to keep up, these islands appeared 'knots of paradise.' The river below Irebu also broadened out so much that, as he says, it might have been a hundred miles in breadth, and was capable, although so widely distributed, of floating the most powerful steamer on the Mississippi. Amina, the faithful wife of Kachéchi, was reported to be dying. On being visited by Stanley, she said : 'Ah, master, I shall never see the sea again. Your child Amina is dying. I have so wished to see the cocoa-nuts and the mangoes; but no— Amina is dying—dying in a pagan land. She will never see Zanzibar. The master has been good to his children, and Amina remembers it. It is a bad world, master, and you have lost your way in it. Good-bye, master; do not forget poor little Amina.' After death, the body of Amina was dressed in its shroud, and at sunset was consigned to the waters of the river.

Passing the heights of Bolobo, the river was studded with

islets, where the natives carried on fishing, and salt-making
from the grasses which grew there.　On the 27th, below Bolobo
and clearing the islets, the river had broadened out into four
miles of clear water.　The natives began to assume a more
civilised aspect.　Arrived at Chumbiri on 27th February, they
received a welcome from the king.　Mr. Stanley gives the
following pen-and-ink sketch of the king: — 'A small-eyed
man of about fifty or thereabout, with a well-formed nose, but
wide nostrils and thin lips, clean shaved, or rather clean
plucked, with a quiet yet sociable demeanour, ceremonious,
and mild-voiced, with the instincts of a greedy trader cropping
out of him at all points, and cunning beyond measure.　The
type of his curious hat may be seen on the head of any
Armenian priest.　It was formed out of close-plaited hyphene-
palm fibre, sufficiently durable to last his life though he might
live a century.　From his left shoulder, across his chest, was
suspended the sword of the bill-hook pattern, already described
in the passages about Ikengo.　Above his shoulder stood
upright the bristles of an elephant's tail.　His hand was armed
with a buffalo's tail, made into a fly-flapper, to whisk mosquitoes
and gnats off the royal face.　To his wrist were attached the
odds and ends which the laws of superstition had enjoined
upon him, such as charm-gourds, charm-powders in bits of red
and black flannel, and a collection of wooden antiquities,
besides a snuff-gourd and a parcel of tobacco leaves.'　The
king took snuff in immoderate quantities, and used a tobacco
pipe which was 6 feet in length, and adorned with brass tacks
and tassels of braided cloth.　The bowl of the pipe was made
of iron, and was large enough to hold half an ounce of tobacco.
The women of Chumbiri attracted the attention of the young
explorer; pretty, many of them of a rich brown colour, large-

eyed, and with a graceful curve of shoulder, they were such as he had not often observed. Many of them were in the habit of wearing brass collars, the weight of which in some cases must have been 30 lbs. Mr. Stanley estimated that his wives must wear 800 lbs. of brass round their necks until death; his six daughters, 120 lbs.; and his favourite female slaves, 200 lbs. On being asked what he did with the brass on the neck of a dead wife, he smiled and drew his finger across his throat in a significant manner, plainly indicating that they were decapitated. After seeing five hundred African chiefs, Mr. Stanley leaves it on record that the King of Chumbiri is the most plausible rogue of all Africa.

Leaving the friendly people of Chumbiri on 7th March, the onward course of the expedition was continued. A rapid river, about 250 yards wide, having two mouths, was discovered; it was named the Lawson river, after Mr. Edward Levy Lawson. The tea-coloured waters of the Ikelemba river, it was remarked, did not mingle with the waters of the Livingstone until they had both flowed side by side for about one hundred and thirty miles, or near Bolobo. It had changed the Livingstone from a clear whitey-grey colour to a deep brown. A river, the Nkutu, issuing from east-north-east, and 450 yards wide at the mouth, was passed on 9th March. This Stanley regards as the Coango, or Kwango of the Portuguese, the sources of which were crossed by Livingstone in 1854. Six miles below the mouth of this river the expedition had encamped near a thick grove to cook breakfast; fires were kindled, and Stanley and Frank were awaiting the cook's voice to acquaint them that breakfast was ready. Suddenly the camp was startled by the report of firing, and six of the men fell wounded. A desperate fight began, when the savages were eventually beaten off, leaving fourteen of Stanley's men wounded. This was the last fight, in all the thirty-second, since entering on the waters of the Livingstone. On the 12th, the river, which had previously narrowed down to 1400 yards, now expanded to 2500 yards, into a lake-like stretch of water, with sandy islands rising in front like a sea beach, and on the right a long row of cliffs extended along the river side. This lake-like expansion, extending from these cliffs, which Frank Pocock suggested should be called Dover Cliffs, to the first cataract of the Livingstone Falls, they termed Stanley's Pool. On 12th March they encamped just above the Livingstone Falls. They were visited here by Itsi, king of Ntamo, who supplied them with cassava pudding, tubers of cassava, bananas, sweet potatoes, sugar-cane, fowls, and a diminutive goat. They refused the liberal bundle of cloths offered to them in exchange. Itsi explained that he wanted only a big goat connected with the expedition; if he had that, he would be satisfied. This goat was the last of six couples purchased in Uregga for presentation to an English lady in accordance with a promise made four years previously. An ass was offered in place of the goat, but the chief growing sulky, Stanley at last consented. He received three smaller goats in return.

After leaving Ntamo, the character of the river began to change. It now rushed vehemently along a steep bed obstructed by reefs of lava, projections of rock, lines of large boulders, and abounding in rapids, cataracts, and falls. Its general feature was that it rushed and roared through a deep, yawning pass from a broad table-land down to the Atlantic. As the river became wilder, the people seemed to become tamer and more approachable, and willing to trade.

The Gordon-Bennett river was reached on the 15th of March, and they found it to be an impetuous stream 75 yards wide; here they prepared to pass at the lower end of the first Livingstone cataract, overland, by means of a brush-covered road. Of the three Livingstone cataracts, this was called the 'Father,' and proved to be the wildest stretch of water Stanley had ever seen. It was like 'a strip of sea blown over by a hurricane.' 'There was,' he says, 'first a rush down into the bottom of an immense trough, and then, by its sheer force, the enormous volume would lift itself upward steeply, until, gathering itself into a ridge, it suddenly hurled itself 20 or 30 feet straight upward, before rolling down into another trough. If I looked up or down along this angry scene, every interval of 50 or 100 yards of it was marked by wave towers— their collapse into foam and spray, the mad clash of watery hills, bounding mounds, and heaving billows; while the base of either bank, consisting of a long line of piled-up boulders of massive size, was buried in the tempestuous surf.' In passing this cataract by hauling the canoes overland, several accidents took place. Mr. Stanley himself tumbled into a chasm 30 feet deep between two large boulders, but escaped with a few bruises. In passing a bad piece of river called the 'Cauldron,' two canoes were lost. On 28th March a terrible catastrophe took place; nine men were lost over the falls, afterwards called Kalulu Falls, from the name of Kalulu, who was one of those who perished there. The falls were cleared by 1st April, when they camped on the right bank below them. On the following day they descended a mile and a half of rapids, when another canoe was lost, reducing their number to thirteen vessels. On 3d April they descended another mile and a half of rapids, during which Stanley narrowly escaped drowning.

One canoe was upset, containing fifty tusks of ivory and a sack of beads. Four men also narrowly escaped drowning. When approaching rapids, the route of the expedition was taken overland, where a broad track was strewn with bushes over which to haul the canoes. On the 10th the *Lady Alice* had a narrow escape from being rendered a complete wreck, getting jammed between two rocks at the entrance to Gavubu's Cove. The lower end of the latter cove was reached on the 11th, and a series of rapids were passed, down which the *Lady Alice* was drifted to the peril of those on board. This danger passed, they encamped at Nkenke Bay, where the waters of the Nkenke, in the shape of a cataract, poured themselves into the Livingstone. Stanley now began to contrast the waters, wild with rapids and cataracts, with the calmness of the upper reaches of the river. From the 16th March to the 21st April inclusive, the expedition made only thirty-four miles, during which they experienced many difficulties and mishaps. During the 22d and the 23d they descended from Nsougu, a distance of five miles, to below Rocky Island Falls, and the next three days were occupied in descending a six-mile stretch to Inkisi Falls. These falls, we are told, have no clear drop; 'but the river, being forced through a chasm only 500 yards wide, is flanked by curling waves of destructive fury, which meet in the centre, overlap, and strike each other; while below is an absolute chaos of mad waters, leaping waves, deep troughs, contending watery ridges, tumbling and tossing for a distance of two miles.' The natives from the neighbourhood crowded around the members of the expedition, expecting to see something extraordinary happen should they venture to go over the rapids. Instead of this, however, Stanley ordered that the canoes be hauled up the mountain beside the falls, and afterwards pass over the table-land. That this was a work of no small difficulty may be learned from the fact that the height was 1200 feet, and that two or three of the canoes were of heavy teak, over 70 feet in length, and weighing over three tons.

Stanley and Frank Pocock began to be in want, like the prodigal son in the parable. Their stores of those luxuries of civilisation, tea, coffee, and sugar, had come to an end. Stanley's last pair of boots were worn out, and long ago Frank Pocock had been wearing sandals made of a leather portmanteau, but often also appeared with bare white feet, for which Mr. Stanley reproached him. It required some generalship to induce the native to compound a more savoury mess than usual of cassava, ground nuts, pea nuts, yams, or green bananas.

While the canoes were being transported by the help of Manwa Sera and neighbouring chiefs over the ground between Inkisi Falls and Nzabi, Stanley explored the neighbouring forests, making jottings of the remarkable trees which fell under his observation ; and choosing two fine trees, well adapted for his purpose, had them cut down and transformed into canoes to replace those he had lost. The largest canoe, of teak-wood, 54 feet long and over 2 feet wide, was launched on 22d May. The chief of Nzabi was well rewarded for the assistance rendered to Stanley with gifts of goods far exceeding his hopes. In passing the falls of Mowa, the *Lady Alice* had her bottom stove in. The whole expedition, journeying partly by land and partly by water, had safely passed the great Mowa Falls by the 27th. On this day it was discovered that Uledi, the coxswain, one of the most devoted of Stanley's followers, had stolen a quantity of beads from their already

impoverished store. Uledi was one of the first-class men of
the expedition, and up to that time had saved thirteen persons
from drowning. It was proved against him. At the close
of the trial, young Saywa stepped forward, and kneeling,
seized his feet and embraced them, saying: 'The master is
wise. All things that happen he writes in a book. Each
day there is something written. We black men know nothing,
neither have we any memory. What we say yesterday is
to-day forgotten. Yet the master forgets nothing. Perhaps,
if the master will look into his books, he may see something
in it about Uledi. How Uledi behaved on Lake Tanganyika;
how he rescued Zaidi from the cataract; how he has saved
many men, whose names I cannot remember, from the river,
Bill Ali, Mabruki, Kom-Kusi, and others; how he worked
harder in the canoes than any three men; how he has been
the first to listen to your voice always; how he has been the
father of the boat-boys, and many other things. With Uledi,
master, the boat-boys are good and ready; without him, they
are nothing. Uledi is Shumari's brother. If Uledi is bad,
Shumari is good. Uledi is my cousin. If, as the chiefs say,
Uledi should be punished, Shumari says he will take a half
of the punishment, then give Saywa the other half, and set
Uledi free. Saywa has spoken.'

'Very well,' I said. 'Uledi, by the voice of the people, is
condemned; but as Shumari and Saywa have promised to take
the punishment on themselves, Uledi is set free, and Shumari
and Saywa are pardoned.'

Uledi, upon being released, advanced and said, 'Master, it
was not Uledi who stole; it was the devil which entered into his
heart. Uledi will be good in future, and if he pleased his master
before, he will please his master much more in time to come.'

The Babwende tribe at Mowa were liberal and hospitable, but easily aroused to the fighting pitch, and very superstitious. Having remarked that Stanley used a note-book for observations, and in order to note down many native words, they ascribed some evil power to its use, and, assuming a hostile appearance, asked him to burn it. If he did not do it, the country would waste, their goats die, their bananas rot, and other evils would come upon them. Our explorer very cleverly substituted a copy of Shakespeare, Chandos edition, and burnt it instead of his note-book, to the immense relief of the people. The neighbourhood of Mowa was rich in bees-wax, about a hundredweight having been discovered clinging to a lofty fragment of rock near Massassa Falls. India-rubber and gum copal were also plentiful. One of their very curious customs was the firing of a gun to announce a death; six shots announced a child's death, ten that of a woman, and fifteen that of a man. The firing is directed at the bananas and palms, their belief being that the death has been caused by bad bananas or a fault in the palm juice.

The Zinga Falls lay two miles below Mowa; and half-way between, the Edwin Arnold river descends 'in a long cascade-like descent, with a sheer drop of 300 feet' into the Livingstone. Its width is 50 yards, with an average depth of 3 feet. The evening of 2d June Stanley spent, as usual, with Frank Pocock beside him in his tent. Although suffering from virulent ulcers in his feet, Frank was unusually cheerful that night, while repairing tattered clothes, and the other odds and ends which needed repairing connected with the expedition. He sang loudly and well many a song or hymn which he had learned in Rochester Church. They had now been thirty-four months together, and the servant, as Stanley remarked, had long ago merged into the companion.

The 3d day of June was a sad one for the expedition, for on that day Frank Pocock and other three men were drowned in endeavouring to descend the falls of Massassa. Having halted seven days at Mowa, Stanley prepared to leave Mowa for Zinga, to establish a camp above its great cataract. One party, consisting of the women and children, and sixty men, carrying the stores, tents, and equipments, were to travel the three miles by land. Another party, consisting of the boat's crew, were to pick their way carefully down the river, and, on coming to Massassa, were to judge as to their ability to pass the falls. Frank Pocock, being an invalid, was to remain behind until a hammock and six men should be sent to carry him. Stanley arrived at a point above Zinga Falls in the afternoon. Four kings were present, and hundreds of natives, all anxious to see him. A hammock and breakfast for Pocock were sent at 1 P.M. In the meantime, Frank Pocock had disobeyed orders, and entered the canoe which was to make down the river. When they reached the head of the falls of Massassa, Frank made light of the difficulties of passing down the falls, in spite of the decided opinion of Uledi that they could by no means do it and live. He was the means of inducing them to attempt the falls of Massassa, taunting Uledi and his men that they were afraid. The result was that they were hurled irresistibly downward, and plunged headlong among the waves and the spray of the falls. Eight of them escaped alive, and amongst those who perished was Frank Pocock. Ndala, the chief, and many of the natives, sympathized with the young explorer in this terrible calamity. They offered him palm-wine, and showed him all the sympathy they could. His own followers, the Wangwana, seemed to grow benumbed, stupid, and apathetic under the calamity. Stanley's own feelings are expressed in these words :—' As I looked,' he says, ' at the empty tent, and the dejected, woe-stricken servants, a choking sensation of unutterable grief filled me. The sorrow-laden mind fondly recalled the lost man's inestimable qualities, his extraordinary gentleness, his patient temper, his industry, cheerfulness, and his tender friendship; it dwelt upon the pleasure of his society, his general usefulness, his piety, and cheerful trust in our success, with which he had renewed our hope and our courage ; and each new virtue that it remembered only served to intensify my sorrow for his loss, and to suffuse my heart with pity and regret that, after the exhibition of so many admirable quali-ties, and such long, faithful service, he should depart this life so abruptly, and without reward.' And so Stanley sat for hours upon a warm boulder near the Zinga Falls, looking upwards towards the treacherous Massassa, hoping against hope that it might not be true, and that he might have escaped. Confirmation of the fact was received, however, eight days afterwards. A fisherman, skimming a certain pool at Kilanga for whitebait, was horrified to witness, floating upon the water, the upturned face of a white man.

After great labour, by 19th June all the canoes were safely brought down to Zinga, past the dreaded Massassa. These operations had been seriously hindered at first by a mutiny amongst some of the men, who declared that they would rather hoe for the heathen than follow him, as the end of it would surely be death. A body of them left the camp, and were only made to return by using force. On 23d June, the new canoe, the *Livingstone*, was carried over the Zinga Falls, and the chief carpenter, who was in it at the time, was drowned. By 25th June, all the canoes of the expedition were safely beyond Zinga. 'A month ago,' he enters in his journal, 'we descended the Upper Mowa Falls; it is still in sight of me, being only three miles off. Three miles in thirty days, and four persons drowned even in this short distance.'

With great danger to themselves, the *Lady Alice* and her crew shot the Mbelo Falls. These rapids were as dangerous as those which the *Lady Alice* had sped down on a previous occasion. Kelanga reached, the danger of famine impelled them towards the sea coast. Mpakambendi was reached on 6th July. Here the river assumed a milder aspect, being less hampered by boulders and cliffy narrows. The foot of Nseuga · Mount was reached by 10th July. Then Nsovoka was reached, and afterwards Lukalu. The warlike district of Kakougo was reached on 13th July, when a market was held below Matunda Falls; where bananas, pine-apples, guavas, limes, onions, fish, cassava bread, ground nuts, palm-butter, earthenware pots, baskets, and nets, were given in exchange for beads, wire, guns, powder, and crockery. The falls of Ntombo Mataka were passed on the 16th July with the assistance of the natives, the Mtombo Mataka, which Mr. Stanley holds to be the politest people he had met with in Africa. By the 20th July, they had descended to the Mata river, where they found that the natives would not part with food except at extravagant prices. They employed themselves chiefly here in whitebait and minnow catching. On 25th July, Safeni, one of his followers, went mad with joy at the news that they were not far from the sea. He said, 'We have reached the sea! We are home! we are home! We shall no more be tormented by empty stomachs, and

accursed savages! I am about to run all the way to the
sea, to tell your brothers you are coming.' And he did run
off to the woods, and was never more heard of. Kilolo was
reached on 28th July. The gallant explorer was now way-
worn and weary. 'The freshness and ardour of feeling with
which I had set out from the Indian Ocean had, by this time,
been quite worn away. Fevers had sapped the frame; over-
much trouble had strained the spirit; hunger had debilitated
the body; anxiety preyed upon the mind. My people were
groaning aloud; their sunken eyes and unfleshed bodies were
a living reproach to me; their vigour was now gone, though
their fidelity was unquestionable; their knees were bent with
weakness, and their backs were no longer rigid with the vigour
of youth, and life, and strength, and fire of devotion. Hollow-
eyed, sallow, and gaunt, unspeakably miserable in aspect, we
yielded at length to imperious nature, and had but one thought
only—to trudge on for one look more at the blue ocean.'
After a tolerably long stretch of calm water, they reached the
district of Kilolo. Here some of his followers roused the
wrath of the natives through stealing cassava and beans.
Three of them were taken prisoners, and six of his men were
wounded. Ali Kiboga, one of those who had been taken
prisoner, afterwards made his escape towards the coast, when
he reached Boma. From Boma he was sent to Kabinda, and
thence to Loanda. From the latter place he was taken to
St. Helena, and thence by one of Donald Currie's steamers,
gratuitously, to Cape Town. He was afterwards wrecked when
on board the *Kaffir*, bound for Zanzibar, but was rescued.

By 30th July the cataract of Isangila was reached. The
supplies received here from the natives of Mwato Zinge,
Mwato Wandu, and Mbinda, were scarce and dear. They

here received the good news that Embomma was distant five days' journey. After deciding in his own mind that he had now unmistakeably proved that the great river of Livingstone had been connected with the Congo of Captain Tuckey, Stanley abandoned the river route, and decided to make the remainder of the journey overland. The joy amongst his men was great at this news. On the 31st July the *Lady Alice* was carried to the north of the falls and left there. The following is the biography of the boat : ' Three years before, Messenger of Teddington had commenced her construction ; two years previous to this date, she was coasting the bluffs of Uzongora on Lake Victoria ; twelve months later she was completing her last twenty miles of the circumnavigation of Lake Tanganyika ; and on the 31st July 1877, after a journey of nearly 7000 miles up and down broad Africa, she was consigned to her resting-place above the Isangila cataract, to bleach and to rot to dust.' The expedition was in a miserable condition when it left Isangila on 1st August. Many were ill with dysentery, ulcers, and scurvy ; their food was scanty and bad, and they were weary and heart-sick.

Reaching the village of Nsanda, permission was received from the chief to send two of his men, accompanied by three from the expedition with a letter to Embomma for relief. The letter explained the miserable condition of the one hundred and fifteen souls, — men, women, and children, — and asked supplies of food and cloth. Within two days the fainting spirits of the men were revived by the return of the messengers with relief from the agents of Hatton & Cookson, the English Factory, Embomma. A procession of carriers brought provisions, cloth, rice, fish, tobacco. With profoundest gratitude, Mr. Stanley found, on going to his tent, that the luxuries of civilisation had not been forgotten. Supplies of pale ale, sherry, port wine, champagne, several loaves of bread, two pots of butter, tea, coffee, white loaf sugar, sardines and salmon, plum-pudding, currant, gooseberry, and raspberry jam. On the 999th day of his departure from Zanzibar, he was met and feasted by a deputation from Embomma, offered the freedom of Boma, and warmly congratulated on the successful completion of his journey. And so the wearied men staggered into Embomma, where they were well fed and cared for. During his two days' stay, three banquets were given in his honour.

Little remains to add. Leaving Boma in the steamer *Kabinda*, they called at Kabinda, and received a cordial welcome from Messrs. Phillips, Wills, Price, and Jones. The change upon the Wangwana, from a life of trial and hardship to one of ease and comfort, had a very depressing effect, and many of them took ill in consequence. The expedition, after an eight days' stay at Kabinda, was embarked on board a Portuguese vessel for San Paulo de Loanda; the utmost courtesy and kindness were experienced from the Portuguese officers towards Stanley and his men. Next embarking on board the *Industry* for the Cape of Good Hope, they arrived there on 21st October. After receiving the kindest attentions there, on the 6th November they again embarked for Zanzibar, arriving there on 26th November. The arrival home of the Wangwana was the signal for every demonstration of happiness. After settling with the survivors of the expedition, and going through an affecting parting with his men, Mr. H. M. Stanley sailed from Zanzibar for Aden on 13th December. The men shook hands with him twenty times at parting, he believed. 'Rapidly, as in some apocalyptic vision,' he writes, 'every

scene of strife with man and nature through which these poor
men and women had borne me company, and solaced me by
the simple sympathy of common suffering, came hurrying across
my memory ; for each face before me was associated with some
adventure or some peril, and reminded me of some triumph or
of some loss. . . . For me, too, they are heroes, these poor
ignorant children of Africa ; for, from the first deadly struggle
in savage Ituru to the last staggering rush into Embomma,
they had rallied to my voice like veterans, and in the hour
of need they had never failed me. And thus, aided by their
willing hands and by their loyal hearts, the expedition had
been successful, and the three great problems of the Dark
Continent's geography had been fairly solved.'

Mr. Stanley received an enthusiastic reception from the
Royal Geographical Society, London, and delivered lectures
on the work which he had accomplished in various parts of
the country. With his customary energy, the account of his
travels was written and published within a few months after
his arrival in this country.

Mr. Stanley has since acted as the leader of a Belgian
International Expedition to the Congo. This expedition is
of a scientific, industrial, and commercial nature, thoroughly
equipped with materials for constructing houses; possessing
wooden huts, tents, provisions, arms, and general merchandise.
The expedition attempts to form temporary or permanent
stations on the banks of the river, and is accompanied (1879)
by men of all trades likely to be of service.

MAJOR SERPA PINTO.

THE journey performed by Major Pinto across Africa in a south-eastern direction, from Benguela to Natal, during 1877-79, entitles him to take high rank as an adventurous and successful traveller. This journey, undertaken for the sole purpose of geographical investigation, was under the auspices of the Portuguese Government. Immediately upon his return to Lisbon on 7th July 1879, Major Pinto took an early opportunity of laying before the chief geographers in London, Paris, and Brussels, the details of his remarkable journey. He appeared at the meeting of the British Association held at Sheffield in August, reading a paper in the Geographical section. In a letter submitted to Lord Northbrook, President of the Council of the Royal Geographical Society, on 16th July 1879, he gave a brief narrative of his travels, of which we present a condensed account.

Starting from Benguela, on the Atlantic coast, Major Pinto reached Bihé, a native settlement in the interior, notifying as he went the position of rivers, mountains, and villages, the chief of which, subject to Portuguese rule, are Quillengues and Caconda. In May 1878 he left Bihé, travelling east-south-east, with a view of reaching the Zambesi, and determining its hydrographical system. The country which forms the southern limit of the Benguelan highlands he found stood 5000 feet above sea level, and was well adapted for purposes of agriculture. Indeed, this is the district which of all tropical Africa he considers best adapted for European colonization. After leaving Bihé, owing to circumstances alien to the wishes of the Portuguese Government, his journey had to be performed on his own resources, he and his party supporting themselves by hunting, with occasional help from friendly natives. His hunting exploits and adventures are fully related in the book of travels which he has published.

Before reaching Bihé, Pinto found the Cubango river taking its rise to the west of that place, instead of to the east, as usually stated. This river receives on the east a great affluent, the Cuito, which unites its waters with the Cubango at a place called Darico. The Cuando, called Chobe by Livingstone, takes its rise east of the river Cuito, in latitude 13° and longitude 19° E. Pinto terms it a fine large navigable river, watering a great extent of inhabited and fertile country. The Cuando also receives several great affluents as navigable as itself. It was in this region, covered in with forests, where the elephant still abounds, that Major Pinto met the Mucassequeres, a tribe of Ethiopian origin, of a yellowish-white colour. They are described as nomadic, and perfectly savage, spending their time in wandering continually in the region between the Cuando and the Cubango.

In his remarks before the Geographical section of the British Association, he mentioned another strange example of the mixture of races he found in a people who, though black, had Caucasian features, many of whom, but for their colour, would have been considered great beauties in this country.

The Bihé district was inhabited, he said, by a mixed race who had come there about a hundred years ago for elephant shooting, and who were as pure Africans as were the Zulus of the south. There the dwellings were square in shape, a sure sign of some civilisation. Their cooking was good, and so well could they work in iron that they converted for him a number of iron hoops into rifle balls. Their courageous character was exemplified by the fact that they sometimes went to hunt elephants with bows and arrows, the latter having reed shafts. The Major also gave an amusing account of the coiffures of both men and women. A beauty in Bihé, it appeared, takes about four or five days to complete her coiffure, but then it lasts about six months.

The country above mentioned is very fertile, inhabited as it is by people of a docile character, susceptible of development, and remarkably fond of dress, which Major Pinto considers augurs well for the after consumption of European manufactures. They are governed absolutely by independent rulers, and although belonging to different races, they constitute confederations. No missionary had been amongst them, and Major Pinto, who was well received, was the first European they had seen. In travelling eastward the Liambi is the first river met with beyond the Cuando. Livingstone had previously visited this river. Between the 16th parallel of latitude and the Victoria Falls, a distance of 220 geographical miles, the river has seventy-two cataracts and rapids. Livingstone had predicted the extinction of the Makololo tribe in this part of Africa, and Major Pinto was able to confirm and verify this prediction: it is this same people, he remarks, bearing the name of Makololos, in former times so brave, and later on so weakened from the effects of fevers in the marsh lands of the

Chobe and Zambesi, abased by licentiousness, and enfeebled by the use of *bang*, who are at last put to death by the assegais of the Luinas. The Makololo race has thus ceased to have a separate existence. Whilst on the Zambesi, Major Pinto had an opportunity of meeting Mochuana, who had been Livingstone's companion on his journey to Loanda, and to this man he owed his life.

South of the Zambesi and the Cuando, the land surface of the country exhibited a rich vegetation, but as far as population was concerned was but a desert. In travelling here Major Pinto met a Portuguese naturalist, Dr. Benjamin Bradshaw, a clever sportsman, living principally upon game and in selling his specimens to the dwellers in the Diamond Fields.

In company with the family of a French missionary, the Coillards, who showed him much kindness, the journey was made from the Zambesi to the Bamangwato country, where they visited the famous Makarikari, the enormous basin into which run and are evaporated the waters of many different African rivers flowing from different points. There ends the Botletle, which, he says, is nothing else than the Cubango, after having made its passage through Lake N'gami. Shoshong he found to be the chief town of the Bamangwato. From this place he journeyed to Pretoria, and from Pretoria to Natal, in company with a young English officer, Lieutenant Barker. To the country which he crossed between the Botletle and the Zambesi, he gave the name of Baines' Desert, in memory of Thomas Baines, who had laboured and worked amidst great privations for the exploration of Southern Africa.

THE END.

www.ingramcontent.com/pod-product-compliance
Lightning Source LLC
Chambersburg PA
CBHW030120030726
47498CB00007B/2473